THE
MARAUDERS

THE
MARAUDERS

PATRICK STRICKLAND

MELVILLE HOUSE
BROOKLYN • LONDON

The Marauders by Patrick Strickland

Copyright © Patrick Strickland 2021
All rights reserved
First Melville House Printing: January 2022

Melville House Publishing
46 John Street
Brooklyn, NY 11201

and

Melville House UK
Suite 2000
16/18 Woodford Road
London E7 0HA

mhpbooks.com
@melvillehouse

ISBN: 978-1-61219-926-9
ISBN: 978-1-61219-927-6 (eBook)

Library of Congress Control Number: 2021947520

Designed by Euan Monaghan

Printed in the United States of America

1 3 5 7 9 10 8 6 4 2

A catalog record for this book is available
from the Library of Congress

TABLE OF CONTENTS

For my mother.

INTRODUCTION
THE BORDER IS EVERYWHERE

Borders dot the perimeter of every country and are present wherever you are at any given moment, no matter how far you are from the actual line separating one nation from the next. Borders are physical places, they are imaginary lines, and they are quite often deadly. People live on borders, and people die on borders. Food crosses borders, and people starve on borders. Borders produce profits for some, and borders generate poverty and suffering for most. Borders follow those who cross them. In the airport, near points of entry, and in the backs of police vans: *the border is everywhere*.

I don't remember the first time I set eyes on a border, but it would have been in the late nineties, during a daytrip with my family. We crossed from Texas, where I grew up, to a town south of the Mexican border. It was when I moved to Israel and Palestine, where I worked as a reporter for four years, that I first saw a massive border wall. Known to Israelis as a security fence and to most Palestinians as an annexation wall, the mostly concrete barrier includes guard towers, barbwire, and soldiered checkpoints. Like all borders, Israel's wall not only attracts violence—it is a magnet for clashes between Palestinian youth and Israeli soldiers—but is in and of itself violent. The wall encroaches on Palestinian land, divides families, and crushes livelihoods.

I was fresh from visiting and writing about communities dotting the border between Lebanon and Syria, where militias armed to the teeth geared up for a battle with the Islamic State in Iraq and Syria (ISIS), when I first traveled to Greece in late 2015, at the height of the mass refugee exodus from war-ravaged and economically devastated countries around the Middle East, South Asia, Africa, to Europe. During that trip, I stood on the shores of Skala Sikamineas, a village on the northern tip of the island of Lesbos. There, I stared out at the water—*the border is everywhere*—as emaciated dinghies carried dozens of men, women, and children crossing the choppy waters of the Aegean Sea, all of them with the hope of reaching safety. Some people wore lifejackets, some wore pool floaties, and some had nothing at all. A few days later, I flew back to mainland Greece and headed north. Outside Idomeni, a village on the Greek-Macedonian border, a tent city had popped up. Thousands of people slept in tents or under the purple skies, enduring the elements. Afghans, Iraqis, and Syrians had fled war. Bangladeshis, Pakistanis, and Moroccans had fled poverty. Bonfires blazed from nightfall onward, exhausted bodies and slack faces encircling them, sitting on the wintry earth cross-legged or with blanket-swaddled children in their laps. Smoke rose in the air, wraithlike. I heard, from every direction, hacking coughs, violent sneezing, and both loud and whispered conversations in Arabic, Farsi, French, Punjabi, Urdu, and Swahili. The rank odor of decaying garbage and molding clothing stuffed in soaked knapsacks rode the gusts of wind that swept through the camp. Whether they left home to escape bullets or empty stomachs, one young man told me, they had left home with the most universal of human desires:

to live. Even as borders slammed shut across the Balkans and the rest of Europe, warehousing tens of thousands of refugees and migrants in Greece, people continued to come. SOLIDARITY WITH PEOPLE STRUGGLING IN IDOMENI, a letter tacked to a corkboard in the camp declared, AND ALL THE MIGRANTS WHO ARE BREAKING THE VIOLENT BORDERS OF EUROPE. YOU ARE NOT ALONE IN THIS STRUGGLE.

In late 2019, the number of boats reaching Greek islands from Turkey had hit the highest level since the crisis erupted more than four years earlier. In fact, around the world the number of people displaced across international boundaries had continued to soar. In 2018, the number of refugees and displaced people around the globe hit a record high when the United Nations High Commissioner for Refugees (UNHCR) documented nearly twenty-six million people seeking international protection outside their home country.[1]

Traveling back and forth between Europe, the Middle East, and the United States between 2015 and 2020, I found myself in border communities time and again, always attempting to make sense of the hate and violence that frontiers inspired. Over the course of two years and during several visits to a handful of communities in southern Arizona, I followed the story of militias and vigilante conspiracy theorists taking up arms to keep immigrants, migrants, and refugees out of the United States. Standing up to people who trafficked in fear, conspiracy theories, and violence was no easy task, and it was one that often prompted yet more fear, conspiracy theories, and violence.

Around the world, the border is everywhere, and everywhere you go, there are idealistic dreamers envisioning a world without it. While I researched and wrote this book, I often thought back to a poster I saw in a squat in Exarchia, the central Athens neighborhood where I usually reside. When the global refugee crisis first reached Europe in 2015, I visited several squats popping up in and around the Greek capital, where anarchists and leftists had taken over abandoned buildings and repurposed them to provide safe housing for displaced people and provide an alternative to the overcrowding and decrepitude of life in the refugee camps. Throughout the last five years, I've passed more hours than I can count in such squats, interviewing squatters and refugees, watching films and sitting in on lectures, and observing general assemblies: the process through which squat residents and volunteers make decisions on the basis of consensus. And I've read and photographed too many posters and graffiti slogans to count, but one has stuck with me. THE BORDER IS EVERYWHERE, it read. WE WILL ATTACK THE REASON FOR OUR SUFFERING.

On the brisk morning of November 1, 2018, only a few days before the midterm elections, I sat in Al Jazeera English's office in Washington, DC. The border had defined much of the election season, and US president Donald Trump had turned it into the central issue. A so-called caravan of refugees and migrants, mostly from Central America, was en route to the United States, and Trump repeatedly warned the nation that this constituted a national security threat like none other: an "invasion," he said. Heeding the president's call to arms, militia groups armed to the teeth were flocking south to communities all along the border.

As I did every day during my short time filling in at the network's bureau in Washington, DC, I scanned the Internet for potential stories, looking for some underreported tale from the border, some way to highlight an alternative opinion on what was happening on the southernmost edge of the nation. Then I stumbled across something that caught my eye. Some residents of a small community in southern Arizona, Arivaca, had put out antimilitia signs in front of their homes and businesses. "Border Town Takes a Stand Against Militias," the article's title declared. I clicked on the link and hit play on the video accompanying the text. The reporter narrating, Morgan Loew, had traveled to Arivaca. "Drive down the main drag in Arivaca, and it might look like any small town in Arizona: a general store, a cantina, and some cool old buildings," he said. "But take a closer look, and you're bound to spot something odd. Signs. Antimilitia signs."[2]

Clara Godfrey, a local resident, appeared on the screen. Her hair was long, thick, and straight, framing her sun-tanned face. "We do not want militias," she said. "No."

The television segment explained that militias and vigilante groups had arrived in town and launched a campaign accusing local residents of working with Mexican drug cartels, human traffickers, and people funneling children into child prostitution networks. Three militia and vigilante groups had already arrived in Arivaca, and Godfrey was outraged.

The story lined up neatly with my journalistic interests. I saw in it the tale of a small town fighting back against a flood of extremely dangerous, virulently racist, and heavily armed outsiders who did not have the community's best interests at heart. I started searching for Godfrey's contact information, but it took a while. The phone numbers I found sent me to disconnected lines, to voicemails belonging to people other than Clara Godfrey. I couldn't find an email address anywhere. Then I found her on Facebook. I sent her a message. I typed up a quick note explaining that I'd like to speak to her by phone, if she was able and willing, and highlight her community's efforts to push out militias. A few days passed and she didn't reply. I figured that my message had landed in the "Other" inbox, where messages from non-friends go. I left a comment on one of her statuses, a few sentences explaining that I had seen her on television, hoped to talk to her, and had sent her a message. Two weeks after my first note, she replied. "Hola, Patrick," she wrote, and explained that she hadn't seen my message sooner. She apologized and provided a phone number where I could reach her. "I would like to speak to you," she said. "I am in Green Valley now, and I will be back in Arivaca this afternoon about five. You have a good one. Thank you much. Clara."

The next evening, we spoke for the first time. I asked a handful of questions I'd jotted down in a notebook, and Godfrey explained the town's history—a history that includes a fatal brush with militias, a tragedy that had shattered the community nearly nine years earlier. When we hung up, I booked a plane ticket to Arizona and reserved a rental car. It was only after arriving in town that I realized how complicated the story would be, and that a short feature article crafted for the Internet wouldn't do it justice.

Arivaca's fight was not the isolated struggle of a lone community. It was a flashpoint in a conflict brewing across the nation. Around the United States, President Trump's 2016 electoral victory had breathed fresh life into a white supremacist movement that had been stagnant, although always present, always waiting, for years. The militia movement enjoyed a decades-long history, but its most immediate incarnation traced back to none other than a series of anti-immigrant border patrols conducted by the Knights of the Ku Klux Klan on the country's border with Mexico in the late 1970s. While much of the media and the nation fixed their attention on the white nationalists and neo-Nazis cropping up in Berkeley, Charlottesville, and Portland, among other places, during Trump's first term in office, the militia movement, too, rode the president's coattails. For those willing to take up arms to prevent foreign nationals from entering the country, Trump's hyperfocus on immigration, immigrants, and the border offered a never-before-seen stamp of approval. For decades, federal authorities had sought to stamp out the armed vigilantes and militia groups organizing and causing mayhem in remote pockets around the country, but now they had a voice in the highest office in the United States.

In early 2016, as it became increasingly clear that Trump would face off with former secretary of state Hillary Clinton in the November presidential elections, he accused the Democratic contender of being soft on terrorism and supporting open borders. Still far off from becoming president, Trump's rhetoric had consequences, spurred extremists to action. That was around the time that the Federal Bureau of Investigation learned of three militiamen in Garden City, Kansas, who were planning to bomb mosques and homes belonging to Somali immigrants.[3] Curtis Allen, Patrick Stein, and Gavin Wright prepared to launch the attack—one that, no doubt, would have led to multiple deaths—on November 9, 2016, the day after the US presidential vote. A fourth member of the militia foiled their plans when he tipped off federal authorities, the plot was stopped before it could be enacted, and the men were arrested and charged with conspiracy to use a weapon of mass destruction and conspiracy against civil rights. In April 2018, a federal jury convicted all three, and later down the line, the trio was sentenced to decades behind bars. Ahead of the sentencing, however, the lawyers made a startlingly accurate claim, albeit while trying to secure leniency for their clients. The man responsible for their actions, Stein's attorneys insisted, was Donald Trump, whose rampant Islamophobia, anti-immigrant vitriol, and "rough-and-tumble verbal pummeling" during the 2016 presidential campaign season "heightened the rhetorical stakes for people of all political persuasions."[4] "The court cannot ignore the circumstances of one of the most rhetorically mold-breaking, violent, awful, hateful and contentious presidential elections in modern history, driven in large measure by the rhetorical China shop bull who is now our president," the lawyers representing Stein wrote in their sentencing memorandum.[5]

Kari Schmidt and Tyler Emerson, Wright's lawyers, followed suit. Trump's anti-Muslim hate—broadcast to the world in tweets such as the one in which he falsely claimed "unknown Middle Easterners" had infiltrated a US-bound caravan—had signaled to their client that he needed to take action in order to defend the country from an impending "invasion." "As long as the Executive Branch condemns Islam and commends and encourages violence against would-be enemies," they argued in their client's sentencing memorandum, "then a sentence imposed by the Judicial Branch does little to deter people generally from engaging in such conduct if they believe they are protecting their countries from enemies identified by their own Commander-in-Chief."[6]

If it had happened at the Oklahoma federal building in 1995, when Timothy McVeigh detonated enough explosives to kill 168 people, and if it had almost happened in Garden City in November 2016, I wondered, how could anyone in Arivaca feel safe with the same ilk of hard-liners living next door?

All those years reporting in Europe, the Middle East, and North America inspired my approach to this book. *The Marauders* is the story of one border and the violence it inflicts on everyday people moving and residing on both sides of it, and it is the story of those who seek justice and equity in borderlands. It is not a comprehensive history of the border or of borderland militias but a snapshot of a moment in that history, and a story of resolve and resilience.

THE
MARAUDERS

CHAPTER ONE
THEY WEREN'T HUNTERS, AND IT WASN'T HUNTING SEASON

When thirty-year-old Megan Davern arrived and clocked in for work at La Gitana Cantina on the warm afternoon of August 12, 2018, she spotted a group of men in tattered army-like fatigues sitting at a textured metal table on the back patio. A cluster of patches on their clothing distinguished them from the other customers, as did the equipment—a remote control-operated drone, flashlights, tracking devices—splayed out in front of them. Fastened to their hips were empty gun holsters. "They weren't hunters, and it wasn't hunting season," the bartender told me in an interview that December.

La Gitana, twelve miles from the US-Mexico border, is open 365 days a year. The only bar in town, the orange-and-teal cantina serves as a meeting hub as much as a watering hole. Most days the bar's patrons mirror the hodgepodge that makes up Arivaca's six-hundred townspeople: Mexican-Americans, some with roots in the area stretching back to a time before the border existed; retirees who escaped the ever-glowing lights of places like Phoenix and Tucson and their suburban sprawl; bohemians who migrated a few miles from a now-abandoned hippie colony;

and humanitarian volunteers who put out water and food in the outskirts for migrants traversing the desert and its rugged mountains.

During my early visits to Arivaca, I would sit and watch customers at La Gitana as they sat clustered at tables inside the restaurant and on the back patio. Flannel-shirted hunters in trucker hats shot pool inside, churchgoing ranchers popped in for lunch, and loners stopped by to purchase a bottle of booze for takeaway. Hunters from far-flung corners of the country showed up after early-morning hunting trips. Pinned to the walls were framed photographs, and ball caps and T-shirts for sale. During the day shift, some patrons would crowd up to the bar, putting back draft beers and bottles while the sun still chewed up the world outside. Others drank RC Cola and shot the shit about town gossip. Back in the kitchen a woman would fry up hamburger patties when an order came in. Once, an amateur gold miner, who told me he was fresh from a wrongful prison sentence and living off the money the government paid him to make up for his time behind bars, explained that he had come to town to pan for gold in the shallow creeks webbing in the desert.

Arivaca did not welcome everyone, though, and La Gitana would not open its doors to just anyone. In a town so close to the border, the frontier between the *here* and the *there*— with such differing views on what constitutes safety and humanitarianism, with so many weapons in the hands of ranchers, hunters, and just about everyone else—suspicion soaked the land itself, political divides left one neighbor hating the next, and human rights were a concept that could be weaponized or dismissed altogether. Scotch-taped to the cantina's door, a piece of paper warned unwelcome

patrons against entering: UNWANTED: MEMBERS OF ANY VIG-
ILANTE BORDER MILITIA GROUP, INCLUDING, BUT NOT LIMITED
TO AZ BORDER RECON. DO NOT ENTER OUR ESTABLISHMENT.

Megan Davern belonged to a younger demographic of
new arrivals in Arivaca. She wore a double piercing in her
nose. Born in California, she had led a transient lifestyle
spending stints in places as distant as Australia and Europe
before moving to the border, and heralded a sort of no-non-
sense progressivism that clashed with the country's prevailing xenophobia over immigration. She was well-liked in
Arivaca, had garnered a solid base of loyal barfly customers, and liked to spread her attention across a wide array
of hobbies and passions: running her local meat-cutting
business; going on hikes with her three-legged dog, Hella,
climbing up and down the mountains that hemmed in the
town; doing humanitarian aid work; and rallying friends
and neighbors to take a stand when her new community
faced potentially problematic issues. She had not lived in
Arivaca in 2009, when rogue militiamen gunned down a
local man and his nine-year-old daughter. She had only
learned of the tragic incident after moving to town—her
ex-boyfriend's daughter had gone to school with the slain
girl—but she knew enough about the danger militias and
vigilantes posed to take a public stance. In spring of 2017,
when Tim Foley, leader of the Arizona Border Recon (AZBR)
vigilante group, moved to town, Davern joined a handful
of her neighbors who were organizing to deter the anti-immigrant leader. They printed up T-shirts that read ARIVACA
EMBRACES LOVE on the front and NO MILITIA, NEVER AGAIN
on the back. In May of that year, around the anniversary of
the 2009 killings, Davern joined around fifteen to twenty
Arivacans for a candlelit vigil commemorating the victims.

The hostility displayed toward Foley belied a deeper reality in Arivaca: while many in the community were glad to shoot the shit over beers or invite you to join them in firing up a joint, Arivacans harbored an endemic—almost innate—resistance to outsiders showing up and, as it were with Foley, drawing too much attention to the community. Even for sympathetic reporters, myself included, navigating discussions about the new arrivals involved carefully stepping on tiptoes around the fault line that was the militia presence, always careful not to trigger a response that could end up with the conversation being shut down with sealed lips and furtive side glances.

On that August day, Davern suspected the men on the patio were militia. She approached their table and asked who the men were and what brought them to town. They were Veterans on Patrol (VOP), answered Michael Lewis Arthur Meyer, the group's forty-year-old founder. They had come to disrupt human traffickers, who, he insisted, funneled children into sexual-slavery rings. She nodded as if sympathetic.

Although nervous, she prepared herself to boot the men. She disappeared into the bar and dialed one of the bar owners, asking whether she should kick them out.

Fearing violence, the bosses urged her to hold off. There was no one there to back her up. Better not to risk provoking them, they told her. Davern relented. Eventually, the VOP members paid their tabs and readied themselves to head out. As they settled their bills, Davern asked a question. Were they affiliated with Tim Foley and Arizona Border Recon? They did sometimes work with Foley, Meyer told Davern, she later recalled.

Meyer and his friends went outside, and Davern took a mental note to alert townspeople of their presence in Arivaca. A flustered customer then barreled through the front door and rushed to the bar. He'd just seen a group of men posted up across the street, carrying guns and filming the humanitarian aid office on the corner, he told Davern. *I'm fucking done with this shit*, she thought.

Outside, Meyer narrated a Facebook Live video for his social media followers. The humanitarian groups were knee-deep in child trafficking, he claimed. "In this community itself," Meyer said into his telephone, "a clear majority of them don't have a problem with an open border; that's how bad it's infected this nation."

Davern followed the men outside and approached them in the parking lot. She confronted Meyer. Sunlight spilled onto the pavement, casting shadows across the parking spots. Gusts of wind sent flutters through her dark-blue flower-imprinted dress. "We've got a pretty strict no-militia policy," she began.

"We're not a militia," Meyer snapped. "We're child search-and-rescue; this is not a militia."

"We've heard about you for a long time," Davern said, extending an upward palm as if offering explanation. She clasped her hands again, her gait faltering and her cadence shaky. "You're Mike Meyer, right?"

"Yeah," he affirmed. "We're getting ready to leave. We gave you our business . . . We appreciate it and everything. We'd appreciate it if people would stop aiding the child trafficking and letting these kids cross through the border."

"Anybody who's working with Tim Foley is not a friend of people here," she said.

"Well, we're not with AZBR. They do border security in their own way. We're not with them. We're only with God. At the end of the day that's the only one we answer to. We don't work with the government. We're independent. We're private citizens."

Davern looked away for a moment, and then turned back to Meyer. "But yeah, I'd appreciate if you don't come in anymore."

Meyer barked back. "You won't have our business no more, that's fine," he said, his camera phone still rolling. Davern strode back into the bar, and Meyer turned back to his phone. "We're gonna go south of every one of their humanitarian aid stations, every one of their jugs, every-where you got the flag up, well, we're positioning south. We've got our drone teams."

"We're gonna separate the good from the bad," he declared to his online followers, "instead of letting all these terrorists and child traffickers and these perverts just come up from our backyard." Meyer turned off his camera, and he and his men rode out of town, ostensibly toward the desert.

In Arivaca, word about the armed men spread quickly, making the rounds on social media. Few residents had qualms with firearms—if you were hiking a desert trail and stumbled upon a rattlesnake, a rifle could come in handy—but even fewer liked the idea of outsiders stirring up trouble in town. Several townspeople called Davern and asked if she was all right, asking what exactly had happened. The encounter still loomed in her mind later that evening when a man phoned her at La Gitana. He introduced himself as Terry Sayles, a retired schoolteacher from Washington now living in nearby Green Valley. She was suspicious at first, but she heard him out. He'd seen the video on VOP's Facebook page, and her face was now broadcast all over the Internet. She should expect harassment in the coming days, he told her. *Okay*, she thought. *This guy knows his shit.*

The next afternoon, Sayles made the forty-five-minute drive from Green Valley to meet Davern at La Gitana. The community needed to prepare itself, he warned. Militiamen from around the nation now knew Arivaca. It turned out that Sayles was an amateur sleuth. Back in Washington, he'd kept an eye on the Aryan Nations and local militia outfits. Now, he'd turned his gaze to the militias and vigilantes kicking up dust around southern Arizona.

———

Davern walked away from her meeting with Sayles fearing the bar incident would not be Arivaca's last run-in with the armed men. In the weeks that followed, a slew of vigilante groups and militias passed through La Gitana. Only a few days after La Gitana banned VOP, Meyer and others returned to stir up trouble. Her colleague Rebecca kicked them out, prompting another heated argument.

Then one day in town, Davern spotted something that gave her pause, something she and others would see several times in the following weeks. A massive black BearCat vehicle adorned with a fake machine gun rolled down Arivaca Road, the dusty pavement stretch connecting the community to I-19, which links Tucson to the Mexican border in Nogales.[1] The vehicle didn't belong to Border Patrol, whose SUVs and pickups are painted white and green. Emblazoned on its windshield were the words TAKE

YOUR COUNTRY BACK, although who exactly had stolen the country remained unclear. Sometimes, on her way to work, Davern would spot the vehicle parked at the Arivaca Mercantile, the town's only grocery store and gas station. She found it odd, maybe a bit disturbing, that some townspeople would occasionally climb on top of the vehicle and pose for photos. "I thought it had a very aggressive presence, which I think was the point," she later told me.

When Bryan Melchior and his friends first showed up in La Gitana, Davern appraised him as a chatty man. Melchior prodded her with questions about the border and about immigration, and identified himself as a reporter. Davern didn't yet know that Melchior, a far-right activist and gun advocate, owned the BearCat she'd seen bouncing up and down Arivaca Road. Melchior said he'd come to town to gather evidence of a crisis on the border with the hope of bolstering US president Donald Trump's case for a wall to keep out immigrants. *This is so fucking weird*, she thought. *This guy is bonkers.* After finishing his dinner, Melchior handed Davern his business card and took off. She looked him up and noted his website: BuildTheWallTV. She rang her bosses, and they updated the list of groups banned from the bar to include Melchior and his cohort.

A radical pro-gun activist and a die-hard Trump acolyte, Melchior was fresh from traveling the country with several of his followers. From Salt Lake City to the Florida Panhandle, Melchior and his fellow provocateurs had staged counterprotests at March for Our Lives rallies.[2] At those student-led protests, demonstrators around the nation demanded stricter gun controls in the wake of the mass shooting that killed seventeen people at a high school in Parkland, Florida, in February 2018. The Utah Gun

Exchange, Melchior's company, was an online marketplace for guns, but he had essentially transformed it into a right-wing gun-centric protest group of the kind of people so obsessed with the right to bear arms that they perceived every modest attempt to cut down on mass shootings as the equivalent of government agents kicking down the doors to their homes and hauling off all their weapons.

By the time he first rolled down the pothole-riddled road leading into Arivaca, Melchior had already formed plans to expose the supposed criminal connections of many of the townspeople on BuildTheWallTV. Accusing any vaguely humanitarian-minded Arivacan of ties to criminal drug cartels had already become such a common refrain among both the outsiders flooding town and the right-wingers living in town that the conspiracy theories were gaining currency in the dark crevices of the Internet, on far-right blogs and pro-militia social media accounts that one assumes would have never otherwise bothered to Google a community like Arivaca, one where only a few hundred people lived, and one more than an hour away from the closest city of repute. Arizona Border Recon leader Tim Foley and Jim and Sue Chilton, local ranchers with ties to then president Donald Trump, welcomed Melchior and his cohort in town. In interviews with BuildtheWallTV, Foley and the Chiltons lashed out at Arivacans and local humanitarian groups that worked with migrants and asylum seekers making the dangerous journey across the southern frontier. In Jim Chilton's mind, the pro-militia media groups would stay around to expose the person he feared would eventually assassinate him for speaking his mind on the border. "I am hoping and praying that if they bump me off," Chilton says in

Melchior's video later posted on YouTube, "guys like you and other friends will make enough noise to make it bad for [their] business."[3]

"I see," Melchior replies. "What you're saying is the more that they piss us off, the more of us that there are down there, and this is their number-one travel route for drugs into the United States, and they want as few people in this area as possible."

"Exactly."

"So, if they piss off Jim Chilton, or they knock you off, they figure, well, we're gonna have ten or fifteen other Jim Chiltons down here to get vengeance."

"And the news media."

"They don't like news down here."

"Nope."

"And neither do the townsfolk."

"Correct," Chilton replies with a sigh. The news media wasn't viewed all that favorably, but there was a special hostility reserved for the faux reporters drumming up far-flung support for the militias that were swarming the town—a fact Bryan Melchior would soon learn, much to his frustration.

When Sue Chilton jumps into the conversation, it takes a turn toward the local. Mrs. Chilton lists off a long tally of enemies, people covertly acting to undermine the sanctity and security of the nation and enemies of those calling for heavily militarized borders: the cartels; officials from former president Barack Obama's administration; shadowy and corrupt Border Patrol agents; rip crews robbing drug runners coming across the border; Mexican Americans "pretending to be Americans"; environmentalists and environmental justice groups tracking ecological damage to the lands in the border area; and humanitarians who, in her estimation, de facto worked on the behalf of gangs and cartels. "There are families in town that are the pickup connection for the drug loads and people and whatever else it is," she says. From Arivaca, local families—who had "competed lethally," she insists—carted the drugs north to be distributed around the country. "Some years ago, there was a home invasion and murder associated with a group that was called a militia. It wasn't *really* a militia. It was a competing family operation that wanted control of the northern route. They went into the home—yes, you see what I mean?"

All the pieces come together, and Bryan Melchior appears to have understood what Mrs. Chilton was getting at. "You're saying this was a turf war?"

"Yes, yes, yes, yes."

"Holy cow."

The militia, she explains, "allied with a family in town. I don't want to say this too publicly. They still live here; the ones that won live here, okay? So we have to be just a little cautious about what we say." She continues, unveiling what she says was a plot to cover up the true motivations of the 2009 murders: "So the story had to be changed to, *Oh, it's a militia, these awful people.* It's not what it was . . . See, but we live in the middle of it, so we have to be careful."

"That's right," replies Melchior.

———

On the afternoon of September 5, 2018—only a few days after Melchior had first chatted up Davern—he burst through the door and stormed over to the bar. "Why was I banned from the bar?" he demanded, according to Davern. He held up his phone, filming the exchange. "I'm not militia."

I don't want to deal with this shit, Davern thought. *Look at this big, gun-toting hothead.* "Hold on," she warned him. "The owners aren't here."

A customer sidled up to the bar and interjected. Melchior didn't have permission to film anyone in La Gitana, the man told Melchior. After all, no one had signed a release, he added.

"Whatever," Davern told Melchior. Then she caught a glimpse of something in Melchior's hand, a bottle of Mike's Hard Lemonade he'd brought from the corner store across the street. "And you can't have an open container from outside in here."

Melchior finally left the bar, but Davern worried that things were getting out of control. Rumors about the militias swept through town, and a meeting was called. Clara Godfrey, who had spent much of her life in Arivaca, had also caught wind of the news. Godfrey didn't take lightly the arrival of militias: her nephew, Albert Gaxiola, had been convicted for participating in a deadly 2009 home raid, and she had weathered years of accusations that she had known in advance about the group's plans—claims she dismissed. (In town, some people continued to promote the idea that Godfrey had been involved, but in my three years visiting Arivaca and southern Arizona, no one ever provided any evidence to support that claim.)

Born in 1960, Godfrey grew up in southern Arizona. She now owned a plot of land, a small corner across from the Mercantile and La Gitana. In the 1990s, she used the land to host matches in her fairly profitable cock-fighting business, back before Arizona banned the sport in 1998—but she now leased part of it to the humanitarian aid office and the local artist cooperative, behind which she lived in a cramped travel trailer. She was affable and lighthearted, enjoyed drinking and having a good time, and found peace smoking late-afternoon joints, the sun sagging behind the mountains and casting a pink-and-purple shroud across the sky. She often said the world rewards and punishes a person according to their juju, but she harbored little patience for the vigilantes and militias setting up shop in Arivaca. For several years a few local right-wing rabble-rousers and militia types had accused her of having links to Mexican drug cartels. When Sue Chilton fingered "a family in town" supposedly working for a cartel, Clara Godfrey knew who she meant: Clara Godfrey. She found the allegations both laughable—she simply points to the fact that she lives in a camper trailer—and enraging. After all, she told me, her family had to live with the hurt of knowing one of their own participated in a brutal murder of two of their own neighbors: a father and small child.

Shortly after returning from a summer trip to Alaska, she spotted the BearCat rattling past Arivaca Mercantile, past La Gitana, and past the US post office next to it. She burst out laughing. "Everything was fake, but it was still there and out there," she told me in December 2018. "It was like a big joke when they brought it out . . . They're driving this big ol' army tank with a big gun on top, all like they're somewhere far away, in a faraway land fighting a big monster."

It was September 6, 2018, the day after Megan Davern ejected the Utah Gun Exchange's Bryan Melchior from La Gitana Cantina. Nearly a month had passed since she'd banned Meyer from the bar, and he was heading a truck carrying a few VOP members back to confront the staff. The sun blazed, and the sky was a deep blue. Riding shotgun, Meyer filmed a Facebook livestream on his cell phone as another VOP member drove down Arivaca Road. They parked in the far corner behind the Mercantile, hopped out, and walked together toward the road, the dusty ground thrumming beneath their feet. They reached La Gitana, and Meyer zoomed in on the sign listing the banned militia and vigilante groups. He pounded on the door. "It's open," said a woman who came to the door.

"Yes, ma'am—I support Arizona Border Recon, Three Percenters, and Oath Keepers," Meyer said. "Am I allowed to come in?"

The woman, wearing an apron and a hairnet, looked confused. She halfway shook her head and then stopped herself. "Uh, let me talk with the bartender," she replied. "I'm not sure."

Rebecca, the bartender on shift, appeared in the doorway. She wore jeans and a steel-blue T-shirt that revealed a cluster of black-and-grey tattoos on her arms. "What's up?" she said.

"Are our supporters—that support us and Arizona Border Recon and everybody—are they permitted to come to this establishment?"

"Utah Gun Exchange is *not* allowed to come in here, nor is Veterans on Patrol." Across her face stretched a tight smile, the kind you make in a tense situation. Her elbows rested on her flanks, her fingers clasped.

"What is the issue with allowing their supporters to come in your business?"

Realizing that Meyer was filming her, Rebecca asked if she had provided him with a release form to film.

"What do I need a release form for?" Meyer shot back. "I'm not media—"

"You're filming me, and I don't want to be filmed."

"I'm an American."

As a private business, Rebecca explained, La Gitana was free to bar anyone they wished from entry. On top of that, only a day earlier Meyer's pals in Utah Gun Exchange had showed up looking for a confrontation, entering the bar with open containers and breaking both state law and La Gitana's rules, she said.

Characteristically confrontational, equipped with a certainty that bordered the religious, Meyer didn't accept that answer. He asked: What about VOP supporters? "Do you stand by your convictions to tell the tens of thousands of supporters—"

The bartender cut him off. "Sure," she said. "Absolutely."

"So you don't want any of our business?"

"Nope."

"We are here to notify you," Meyer said, launching into what sounded like scripted tirade, "that we've already established teams north where your water tanks are, on the routes . . ."

"*Our* water tanks?"

"We're building a wall north of Arivaca . . ."

"Does La Gitana have water tanks?" she asked. The absurdity was setting in. "I'm confused."

"We're building a wall around Arivaca, to the north," he insisted. "We've extended the wall. So, if you guys wanna be with Mexico, you're more than welcome to." Meyer turned to walk off and shouted, "Have a good day, ma'am."

He beelined to the humanitarian aid office across the street; it was, after all, the true reason the militias insisted on building a presence in town. Meyer launched into another tirade, railing against the humanitarians for "helping children, women, and everything else to cross this border illegally."

Throughout the nearly ten minutes that made up the rest of the video, Meyer announced VOP's fever dream plans to "surrender Arivaca and Ruby over to Mexico." His group would block migrants and refugees from moving north and effectively leave them stranded in Arivaca. How a group of around a dozen men could carry out such an operation, he failed to explain. This was "enemy territory," he said, and he wouldn't stand by while people in Arivaca tried to marginalize Tim Foley and the Arizona Border Recon. "You leave AZBR alone," he shouted.

The way he told it, his new plans—"Operation Open Headache," he aptly called it—would include shutting down national parks through which migrants cross, destroying even more water tanks around the southern Arizona desert and besieging Arivaca with a Trump-like wall. As they rode out of Arivaca once again, he fielded questions from his followers on Facebook Live. "We're going to be shopping outside and we're going to see just how much impact we can have on this town when they're stuck with the illegals they're facilitating coming through," he said. "They're going to stop coming through here because these people sure as hell aren't gonna take care of 'em."

Coming to a close, he called on his followers to keep an eye on Arivaca: "That town does not want American patriots—any *American*—coming down through there, but they'll take every illegal crossing up through the south. That ain't right. You ain't my neighbor when you do that; you're not my neighbor. And you're putting children's lives at risk, and then secretly they'll raise donations for those people. Because Lord forbid, if people found out they were trafficking children, like you don't already know."

His driver spotted something in the rearview. "We've got a tail," he warned.

"That's all right," Meyer replied. "Let 'em tail us."

———

On September 9, 2018, around sixty people crowded into the historic little schoolhouse in Arivaca, situated at the helm of the home-dotted field behind the Arivaca Mercantile. Clara Godfrey, her suntanned face framed by her long silver hair, took the lead. Fired up, perhaps fueled by a sense of personal responsibility, she urged the attendees to drive the militias and vigilantes from Arivaca. It didn't matter who these militiamen were, Godfrey said. They were bad people; they needed to leave. Any militiaman— *any* one of them—existed on the same moral plane as the militiamen of the past, the ones that gunned down a family, the ones that killed a child, the ones that shattered a community, the ones that left a generation of children in the town growing up with the fear of a late-night raid, of armed men kicking down the door and shooting dead anyone that stood in their way.

As Godfrey delivered her fiery screed, some people in the crowd jostled nervously. In a town where so many lived by the creed "Live and let live," not everyone would hitch their wagon to a freight train whose conductor advocated such a militant pushback, a resistance so stubborn and so sure-headed that it clashed with the prevailing ethos in Arivaca. Sure, the militias represented something dangerous, but were these armed groups not made up of fellow human beings? Sensing the need to calm the room, Megan Davern stood up and intervened. She explained the situation in detail. She recounted the information that Terry Sayles, who was also present, had explained to her after the first confrontation with Veterans on Patrol at La Gitana. The groups thrived on social media outlets like Twitter and Facebook, she said, where they drummed up an angry rabble of followers and provoked harassment against critics. The town needed to take action, she pleaded, but they also needed a clear plan. By the time the meeting concluded, they had a set of goals. They would start a private Facebook page where they could share information about militia groups and vigilantes in town. They would target the vigilante groups' social media accounts. They would seek injunctions against harassment. And some, only a few willing attendees, would put up antimilitia signs on their property. Godfrey volunteered to put several signs on her land—each of them displaying the word MILITIA circled and crossed out in red paint.

Megan Davern walked away from the meeting feeling hopeful that the townspeople could come together and send a resounding message of defiance. That message would be that as a community, Arivaca would not grant an inch to the militias: the same kind of message that people around the United States were searching for at a time when the president was preaching sulfuric levels of hate for anything considered foreign, anything that could reasonably (or unreasonably) be portrayed as a national threat. But someone delivered Davern a message first.

On September 23, 2018, she woke up and readied herself. She strolled down her driveway, the dirt thrumming beneath her feet, and stumbled upon a plastic water jug. It was the type of water container that humanitarians routinely left behind in the desert for migrants and others making the crossing. A large stone sat on top of it, holding it in place. She bent down for a closer look. Someone had stabbed the container several times.

CHAPTER TWO
A HISTORY OF VIOLENCE

On May 3, 1844, a group of "native" Americans—as these United States–born, anti-immigrant Anglos described themselves—gathered at the main market in Kensington, then Philadelphia's Irish Catholic enclave.[1] Standing there at the intersection of Second Street and Master Street, the crowd attracted a gaggle of suspicious Irish onlookers. The Irish group suddenly rushed the nativists and sent them scattering in all directions. The Irish hurled stones and bottles as they gave chase to their detractors. Humiliated, the nativists vowed to burn down a Catholic church in response to the embarrassment of being driven from their own demonstration.

The following Monday, the nativists assembled in front of a schoolhouse. They raised a flag—likely their signature flag, an American flag bearing the ominous words NATIVE AMERICANS, BEWARE OF FOREIGN INFLUENCE—and cheers erupted. A man called Kramer ascended the jerry-built podium. A storm was brewing above him. Kramer picked up where the abandoned meeting had left off on the previous Friday. Around three thousand supporters, many of them armed with makeshift weapons, had assembled to hear the nativists rail against Catholic immigration to the United States. Tensions were high by the time Lewis Charles Levin, a thirty-five-year-old newspaper owner, climbed atop the stand to address the crowd.

Levin had spent years railing against alcohol, but now his focus had shifted to Catholic immigration, and he nimbly channeled the same fervency he'd employed when speaking about the supposed dangers of booze.[2] It wasn't that giant a leap. Liquor and Catholicism were synonymous in the mind of many nativist agitators and pamphleteers. Levin's political party, the Native American Party, had first appeared in New York a year earlier, and its goal mirrored his own: halting all Catholic immigration to the United States. James Harper, the publisher, was elected on a similar platform to Levin's as mayor of New York, in a "stunning upset" in the month before Levin made his speech.[3] Nativism was in ascendence.

Almost as soon as Levin began speaking, unruly gusts of wind swept through the gathering, and rain pelted the three thousand attendees. Many ran to take cover from the downpour, but the majority reassembled at the neighborhood's main market. There, a swarm of Irish residents ready for a confrontation approached the nativists. Around "twelve or fifteen persons ran out of the market from the west side, pursued by about an equal number," later recounted John B. Perry, who witnessed the day's events unfold in real time. When a fistfight erupted between an Irishman and a nativist, the "two desperate fellows clinched each other, one armed with a brick, and the other with a club, and exchanged a dozen blows, any one of which seemed severe enough to kill any ordinary man."[4]

Perry described bricks and stones that whizzed through the air overhead, and the gunfire that rang out in the market. Many nativists darted away in search of safety. As the Irish gave pursuit, armed with bricks and a few muskets, the nativists fired shots back in their direction. A gray-haired man in a seal cap fired his musket toward the nativists, who then lost their position and were forced to peel off down the street. On Germantown Street, a bullet tore into the chest of teenage nativist George Shifler. His comrades hoisted him up and carried his limp body to a drugstore, but he was already bleeding out. Shifler died within a few moments. Several other brawlers on both sides of the melee were shot—some in the hip, and at least one in the face. People smashed their opponents with lead pipes and bludgeoned them with stones. Homes were raided, looted, and smashed up, left in ruins. "The Irish population were in a dreadful state of excitement," Perry recounted, "and even women and boys joined in the affray, some of the women actually throwing missiles."

When some were gunned down or beaten to death, their allies could not retrieve them. Bystanders and residents fled, and the rage-filled mob targeted many of them with violence. Others took up arms and guarded their homes as fires burned around the neighborhood. Gunshots were fired from home windows, behind fences, and dark alley-ways. It was not until past 1:00 a.m. that the riots faded.

At 3:30 p.m. the following afternoon, the nativists turned up again, this time at State House Yard, a public garden in Philadelphia. The rabble grew impatient as party officials called for adopting peaceful protest and advocacy as a means to secure their anti-immigration objectives. "Adjourn to Second and Master streets now," some screamed, according to Perry. "Let us go up into Kensington."

Although the party president implored them to avoid violence, thousands were soon marching back to the Irish enclave. They waved flags and carried banners. Upon arriving at the market, rioting erupted once more. When gunshots flew from home windows, a nativist hit the ground dead, while several others were injured. By 6:00 p.m. a handful were dead, and others left maimed by gunfire. The sidewalks swelled with men coming back and forth from the street brawls, and rumors of killings swirled throughout the crowds. As the nativists scrambled to retrieve a lifeless cadaver, a salvo of gunfire sent them retreating. They set aflame several homes where they believed Irish gunmen had been firing upon them, beating and mauling the inhabitants rushing from the flames. Implored to act, the sheriff said it would be "futile," Perry wrote, because the mobs were "well armed and desperate, and could only be over-awed by an imposing and active military force."

Firefighters initially refused to approach the burning homes, fearful of being fired upon. With an armed escort, however, a handful of firemen hosed the flames, but by the time the riots died down, the market and several homes had been "reduced to a heap of ashes."

When militiamen swarmed Kensington the following day, they found a neighborhood comprised of charred homes, crumbling structures, and devastated families. In the early afternoon, the crowds swelled once more. Someone set fire to St. Michael's Catholic Church, and the priest escaped with the help of soldiers. As nightfall set in, fires chewed up more homes and churches.

When all was said and done, the nativists had burned down thirty homes and several Catholic churches. At least seven individuals from both dueling mobs had died, and the injuries were too many to ascertain.[5]

Born in 1808 to Jewish parents, Lewis Charles Levin had drifted around the country, graduating from South Carolina College and later teaching in Mississippi. He practiced law in Kentucky and Maryland before arriving in Philadelphia in the 1830s. In 1842, after founding the anti-alcohol *Temperance Advocate* newspaper a few years earlier, he hosted a bonfire in which liquor went up in flames.[6] As Catholic immigration from Germany and Ireland swelled between 1830 and 1860, Levin developed a sinister worldview, one in which Catholics sought to unravel the freedoms won by the American Revolution through infiltrating its democratic processes. Catholic immigrants, he claimed, harbored dreams "of our government changing to a monarchy—when his holiness [the Pope) will have a King ready, sprinkled with holy water, to mount the throne in the name of Catholic liberty!"[7]

Blaming a "ferocious mob of foreigners" for the Kensington violence, Levin "stood alone . . . in his attempt to justify the violence and church burning," said the historian John A. Forman in his seminal 1960 essay on the firebrand politician.[8] Although Levin received the lion's share of the blame for the riots, he weathered the criticism and continued to enjoy a swelling base of supporters. Subsequently running for Congress, he advocated raising the age requirement for naturalization, restricting political office to US-born individuals, and abolishing all forms of foreign influence on American institutions. His "provocative and belligerent"[9] orator's style equipped him to drum up a crowd and a support base that helped land him in office from 1845 to 1851, even though generally the initial burst of nativist fervor faded "back to embers after the elections of 1844."[10] He accused foreign-born Americans with political aspirations of not having been "sufficiently long in the country to have lost the odor of the steerage of the ships that brought them across the Atlantic."[11] The presence of foreign-born voters at polling stations, he claimed, drove "away in disgust many native citizens."[12] Fiercely antagonistic and outspoken, he rode a wave of anti-immigrant hysteria washing over the country.

His party, which eventually merged with others and was rebranded as the Know-Nothing Party—members, when the group was an underground one, were instructed to say that they "knew nothing" if asked about the organization— surged in membership throughout the 1850s, even as Levin himself failed to return to office. In 1851, Levin ran a failed bid for the US Senate, and he was subsequently accused of a spate of attempted briberies.

While the population grew naturally, immigration also continued to swell, and the Irish continued arriving in large numbers in the United States.[13] Many fled famine and poverty and hoped to find opportunity and prosperity in their new country.

Three years later, the Know-Nothing Party swept elections in several New England cities, among them Salem and Boston. In 1854, Philadelphia saw Robert T. Conrad—a candidate for both the Whigs and the Know-Nothings—sweep the mayoral elections, campaigning on promises to bar foreign-born Americans from holding political office and to shutter saloons on Sundays. Within months, the party's membership swelled from tens of thousands to over a million. John T. Towers, who had joined the Know-Nothings in 1852, became the sixteenth mayor of Washington, DC, in 1854, unseating the Democratic incumbent.[14] That same year, all the way across the country in San Francisco, California, a Know-Nothing chapter was born to oppose Chinese immigration. In Chicago, a Know-Nothing candidate, Levi Boone, won the mayoral elections in 1855 and banned immigrants from holding city jobs.[15]

Violence like the kind that struck Philadelphia in May 1844 soared alongside the Know-Nothing Party's popularity. On Election Day in 1855, Protestant mobs swarmed the streets of Louisville, Kentucky. German and Irish Catholics had grown into a sizeable minority in the city—around one-third of the population—and local newspaper writers, influenced by the Know-Nothing Party's ideology, railed against them. Armed and enraged, the mobs prevented Catholics from casting their ballots, taking control of the polls in several wards by sunrise. Newspaper reporters witnessed nativists chasing two foreigners from the voting booth, beating and stabbing them. Bludgeoning and gunning down people in the streets, the mob attacked a Catholic church on Shelby Street. Musket-lugging men torched a brewery, and German-owned coffeehouses were raided and pillaged. When Irish-owned homes went up in flames, at least five people burned alive: "roasted to death," one journalist later observed.[16] "We are sickened with the very thought of the men murdered, and houses burned and pillaged, that signalized the American victory yesterday," the *Louisville Daily Journal* wrote the next day. "Not less than twenty corpses from the trophies of the wonderful achievement."[17]

The bloodshed was too much for Mayor John Barbee, even though he himself was a Know-Nothing. He intervened to save a Catholic cathedral from the approaching mob. By the time the rioting dissipated, at least twenty-two people were dead, more than a hundred businesses and homes were blazed, and flames had chewed up and devoured whole families. The day became known as Bloody Monday. Authorities never prosecuted anyone for the violence.[18]

One of the oldest myths in American history is the notion that racism and discrimination toward newcomers is hypocritical in a country "founded on immigration." In the United States, paranoia-fueled anti-immigrant violence is rooted in the country's establishment as a predominantly white Protestant nation, a process made possible only through the genocide of Indigenous people and the mass enslavement of Africans kidnapped from their homelands and their descendants. Fears of demographic change are imbued by racism, and those fears are embedded in the country's DNA.

Even before the establishment of the United States, colonial settlers, including those who later founded the nation, expressed fear over the immigration of non-Protestants from Europe. The founding father and inventor Benjamin Franklin described German newcomers as "the most ignorant Stupid Sort of their own Nation." Although Franklin did not advocate a ban on immigration, he pushed for tighter restrictions. Fearing that too many Catholic immigrants threatened the white Protestant demographic majority, he added: "The Spaniards, Italians, French, Russians and Swedes, are generally of what we call a swarthy Complexion; as are the Germans also, the Saxons only excepted."[19]

In 1790, nearly fourteen years after the country's independence, the US Congress passed the first naturalization act, restricting naturalization to "free white persons" who had been in the country at least two years and were of "good moral character."[20] In 1795, the bar was again raised higher: applicants needed to have been in the country for at least five years. Another three years later, yet another naturalization act introduced a fourteen-year residency requirement for naturalization applicants.

Throughout the 1800s, anti-immigrant hysteria reared its head time and again—from the Know-Nothing Party to measures designed to bar Chinese immigration to the United States. In San Francisco, California, a so-called vigilance committee formed in 1851 amid growing tension over crime. Along with much of the southwest, California had only become part of the United States three years prior, when the Treaty of Guadalupe Hidalgo ended the Mexican-American War and transferred more than half a million square miles of territory to the United States. The San Francisco Committee of Vigilance was formed in response to criminal activities by the Sydney Ducks, a gang of immigrants from Australia. Nearly half of the Sydney Ducks had been born in Ireland, left for Australia when their home country was struck by the years-long Great Famine in 1845, and then resettled yet again in Northern California, where a gold rush had attracted hundreds of thousands of newcomers. News of gold brought so many to San Francisco that the nine-hundred-person town grew to more than twenty thousand between 1848 and 1851.

Only a day after forming, the first vigilante committee hanged John Jenkins, an Australian immigrant accused of theft and burglary. During the three months following its formation, the vigilantes hanged to death three more. In addition to extrajudicial executions, the mob carried out vigilante patrols, detained and interrogated individuals suspected of crimes, and forcibly deported immigrants. The first committee dissolved during elections in September of the same year, only three months after popping up.

In 1856, another vigilante committee took shape in San Francisco. Like the first vigilance committee, the second manifestation focused largely on criminality and "cleaning up" the city. Anti-immigrant sentiment continued to animate the committee's activities, though, and the group continued to mete out racist violence—particularly against Chinese immigrants—after its formal dissolution three months onward.

———

Owing to a deadly crop failure in southern China in 1852, Chinese immigration to the United States skyrocketed. Most of the new arrivals were males seeking work in manual labor, especially in the mines. In 1852, more than twenty thousand Chinese nationals entered the United States through the San Francisco customs house, compared to the 2,714 who had passed through a year earlier.[21] The spike was so dramatic that Chinese immigrants made up one in five residents of the four counties that constituted California's southern mines. With anger mounting, local authorities sought to appease the white population by clamping down on Chinese workers. In May, the state introduced the Foreign Miners' Tax, a move that imposed a three-dollar monthly fee on foreign nationals working in the mining industry. Rather than pacify the increasingly angry white miners, the introduction of the tax led to violence.

One such instance of violence had a monumental impact on American law. In 1853, George Hall and two other white men attempted to rob a Chinese miner near Bear River, in California's Nevada County. Ling Sing, another miner, tried to intervene, but Hall shot him dead on the spot. Police arrested Hall and charged him with murder, and a jury found him guilty. Sentenced to death by hanging, Hall appealed the conviction, climbing up the legal ladders until eventually reaching the California Supreme Court. He argued that he could not be convicted on the testimony of Chinese immigrants, citing a California law that barred testimony from a "Black, or Mulatto person, or Indian."[22] The law did not mention Chinese or Asian individuals, but Chief Justice Hugh C. Murray, a member of the Know-Nothing party and a vicious opponent of immigration, delivered the majority opinion in favor of Hall. "His zeal for protecting white Americans from the potential harmful influences of inferior races is clear in the language of the majority opinion," the historian Wendy Rouse has written.[23] In 1854, a Know-Nothing chapter was established in California, and its primary function was to oppose Chinese immigration.

The justice system continued its assault on Chinese immigrants, and in 1858, California legally prohibited the immigration of Chinese or "Mongolian" individuals, although they comprised a meager 0.0011 percent of the country's population of thirty-one million. Facing barriers to working in California's mines, many Chinese immigrants sought work on the railroads being built to connect the eastern states to the Western frontier, and immigration continued to grow despite the hurdles.

In 1870, the US Congress approved the Naturalization Act, effectively banning Chinese from being granted citizenship and blocking the legal immigration of Chinese women whose spouses worked in the United States. The following year, anti-Chinese violence hit a fever pitch in Los Angeles. On October 24, 1871, tensions between white settlers and Latinos on the one hand, and Chinese immigrants on the other, boiled over.[24] Disputes over prostitution networks in the city had partially fueled the anger behind the scenes. That night, the mobs hunted down Chinese immigrants in the city, mainly in the Chinese quarter, and gun battles erupted between police officers and Chinese immigrants. By the time the violence dissipated, at least eighteen Chinese immigrants had been tortured and killed, many of them hanged in front of crowds that were applauding the slaughter. When the killings went to trial, the court heard no testimony from Chinese eyewitnesses, whom the law still barred from testifying against white men.

———

In the 1850s, some of the first armed vigilantes to patrol the porous borderlands were on the search for escaped slaves seeking passage into Mexico. While the famed Underground Railroad helped runaway slaves reach freedom in the Northern states or in Canada, another route led them to Mexico, where slavery had been abolished in 1829.

In 1857, Nathaniel Jackson left his home state of Alabama and resettled in Texas's Rio Grande Valley, traveling with several families and formerly enslaved people.[25] Along with his wife, Matilda, who was an emancipated African American, Jackson had hoped to escape the racism and intolerance of the American Deep South. He planned on moving to Mexico. In the end he stopped in San Juan, then a small community just north of the frontier, and established a ranch. In case of danger, he and Matilda knew they could escape across the Rio Grande River and into Mexican territory. Jackson and his family in fact risked a great deal of danger turning their ranch into a safe haven for formerly enslaved people and helping them escape across the country's southern border.

Armed patrols gallivanted along the border, searching for emancipated African Americans and often illegally crossing the border into Mexico.[26] After the abolition of slavery and the triumph of the Union during the Civil War, however, anger over Chinese immigrant workers led to the creation of a new type of border militia. The Mounted Guards, numbering around seventy-five people, operated out of El Paso, Texas, and their primary purpose was to prevent Chinese immigrants from entering the country. Riding on horseback up and down the border from Texas to California, the Mounted Guards patrolled the borderlands for Chinese crossers. They often collaborated with the Texas Rangers and with US soldiers stationed on the frontier.

Anti-Chinese xenophobia and bigotry had been mounting for decades, and the Mounted Guards' foundation came more than two decades after the Chinese Exclusion Act, markedly racist legislation that forbade Chinese immigrants from coming to the United States.

———

In the late 1800s, American politicians increasingly took aim at immigrants and immigration. As waves of immigrants sailed to the country between 1865 and 1890, most of them from northern Europe, Congress sought to introduce new laws restricting who could and who couldn't come to the United States. In 1875, a new law prohibited anarchists, criminals, sex workers, and polygamists, among others, from entering the country. In the two decades that followed, more laws sought to ban entry to those with certain mental health problems ("the insane"), individuals who had certain contagious diseases, and those whom authorities worried would become dependent on government financial aid to survive in the country. Labor laws banned employers from advertising jobs overseas, and immigrants weren't admitted if they had made work contracts before they set foot in the country.

Between the late 1800s and 1915, another surge of immigrants mostly came from eastern and southern European countries, Russia, and Ukraine, among others. Around the time World War I started in 1914, anti-immigrant sentiment was mounting fast. A new string of anti-immigrant laws were introduced. One such law, passed in 1917, required immigrants to be literate, to meet certain physical prerequisites, and to meet a particular economic standard. It also put in place on ban on immigrants from many Asian and Pacific Island countries. Later, in 1921, the United States introduced a quota system that put a cap on the number of immigrants from any individual country. In a single year, the number of immigrants from a particular country could only reach as high as 3 percent of the total number of people from that country who had been living in the United States in 1910. That bar was later lowered to 2 percent.

At around 6 a.m. on December 21, 1919, it was still dark when the *USAT Buford* nodded out of New York Harbor. The ship had recently made several trips to and from Europe, hauling American troops home as World War I came to an end. Now the vessel had a new purpose: to ship 249 immigrants believed to be communists and anarchists to the newly founded Soviet Union. Nearly two hundred of those aboard the ship—dubbed the Soviet Ark by the press—had been swept up on November 7 as part of the Palmer Raids, a series of raids that led to the arrests of thousands of suspected left-wing immigrants—mostly Italians and Eastern European Jews. Hundreds of those detained were eventually deported. "Slowly the big city receded, wrapped in a milky veil," Alexander Berkman, an anarchist writer who was on the *Buford*, later wrote of the departure. "The tall skyscrapers, their outlines dimmed, looked like fairy castles lit by winking stars and then all was swallowed in the distance."[27]

Emma Goldman, a Lithuanian-born Jew, was also aboard the ship. She had immigrated to the United States at sixteen years old in 1885, but she landed on the list of deportees for her prominence as a free speech advocate, labor organizer, and critic of the American government.[28] "Ludicrously secretive were the authorities about our deportation. To the very last moment we were kept in ignorance as to the time," Goldman later wrote of the trip. "For twenty-eight days we were prisoners," she recounted. "Sentries at our cabin doors day and night, sentries on deck during the hour we were daily permitted to breathe the fresh air. Our men comrades were cooped up in dark, damp quarters, wretchedly fed, all of us in complete ignorance of the direction we were to take."[29]

By the time the Palmer Raids ended, the authorities had arrested upwards of 3,000 people and deported hundreds of them. The raids marked the climax of the First Red Scare (1917–1920), a period during which the US government leveraged the feverish patriotism of World War I to sharpen widespread fears of a supposedly impending communist or anarchist revolution. American authorities clamped down on communists, anarchists, immigrants, striking workers, and Black Americans, among others.

———

It was against that backdrop of increasing anti-immigrant sentiment that a prominent conservationist emerged as a leading eugenicist in the early twentieth century. In 1916, the conservationist Madison Grant, born in New York City to a wealthy family tracing its lineage to early colonists, published a book that received little attention at first. Unlike his writings on the moose, the Rocky Mountain goat, or other North American mammals, Grant's *The Passing of the Great Race* examined the supposedly harmful impacts of non-Nordic immigration to the United States.

Grant had gained notoriety as a conservationist and zoologist, but his 1916 ravings on Nordic superiority went on to form an important foundation of anti-immigrant hysteria that gripped the country, in ebbs and flows, ever since. Americans with roots tracing back to Scandinavia, Grant argued, risked extinction at the hands of immigrants supposedly diluting the racial purity of Americans. Unlike the religious and sectarian bents of the Know-Nothing Party's ideology, Grant's theory took aim at those immigrating to the United States from southern European and eastern

European countries. Where the Know-Nothings targeted Catholic Germans, Grant found a favorable audience in Germany: after his book was translated into German, the future Nazi leader Adolf Hitler lifted large passages from *The Passing of the Great Race* and republished them in his autobiographical screed, *Mein Kampf*.[30] His passion for conservation was far from being unrelated to his desire for racial purity; rather, natural resources, Grant argued, must be reserved for the Nordic race.

——

Hit hard by the Great Depression in the 1930s, the United States saw unemployment skyrocket. Even as new arrivals briefly slumped, the government ramped up attempts to decrease the number of immigrants living in the country. Some Mexicans were offered "free" train rides back to their home country, and more than a million US citizens were deported to Mexico during the economic catastrophe.[31]

But between 1933 and 1945, as Nazi Germany rose and, starting in 1941, carried out the Holocaust and invaded and occupied much of Europe, between 180,000 and 220,000 refugees fled to the United States.[32] Mostly Jews fleeing genocide, they were often dubbed "spies" seeking to infiltrate the country on behalf of the very Nazis who were systematically exterminating their people. The United States put quotas in place that kept the number of Germans and Austrians allowed to enter the country at 27,000, a number that didn't take into account whether they were Jewish or not. That didn't matter—American politicians defended the policy in the name of national security, a theme that runs through the country's entire history. "Not all of them are voluntary spies," President Franklin D. Roosevelt said at one point. "It is rather a horrible story, but in some of the other countries that refugees out of Germany have gone to, especially Jewish refugees, they found a number of definitely proven spies."[33]

Anti-immigrant movements cropped up from time to time, some more militant than others, but throughout the second half of the twentieth century, suspicion and fear toward newcomers and outsiders endured as a constant theme of American political life. Throughout the 1950s and 1960s, as Black Americans, other people of color, and anti-racists of all stripes waged a struggle for civil rights, a new crop of far-right groups fought to prevent equity. Inevitably, many far-right militants later trained their sights on immigrants and refugees.

In the late 1970s and early 1980s, Klansmen across the country started patrolling the US-Mexico borders. Louis Beam, a longtime white nationalist, Klan leader, and ideologue behind the so-called lone-wolf terror tactic, was one of several who led efforts to police the border and hunt down immigrants. Although some of the patrols mostly functioned as "publicity stunts," according to the historian Kathleen Belew, they also offered the Klansmen "a way to inculcate real anti-immigrant hostility and encourage acts of violence."[34] Later, David Duke—who decades on became a state lawmaker in Louisiana—and his acolytes drove up and down the border in Southern California with banners that read KLAN BORDER WATCH draped from their cars. Beam, like others, defended the border patrols by arguing that his men were enforcing the very laws of the US government, which, he claimed, was not enforcing immigration restriction and securing the southern frontier.

In 1981, Beam unleashed his followers on Vietnamese fishermen who had come to the country as refugees after the US devastation of their homeland. As tensions between Vietnamese shrimpers and white shrimpers boiled over in Galveston Bay, Texas, Beam delivered a "fiery speech" while a boat with the words USS VIETCONG painted on its side was set ablaze. After his followers were riled up, Klansmen burned crosses in yards of Vietnamese homes in town, a pair of Vietnamese-owned boats went up in flames, and Klansmen "rode a shrimp boat around the bay, displaying a hanging human effigy and firing blanks from a cannon."[35]

In the years that followed, Beam continued to train his followers in paramilitarism. All the later militancy of anti-immigrant militias on the border was embodied in Beam during those formative years of his movement: border vigilantism, anti-immigrant hysteria, and hostility to the federal government, as well as armed activities. It was no surprise that, in 1983, he dedicated his book *Essays of a Klansman* to "those yet unknown patriots, who are even now preparing to strike at the enemies of God, our race and our nation."[36]

Throughout the rest of that decade and the one that followed, border militias cropped up and continued to operate up and down the southern frontier with Mexico, growing in size and strength. Some openly embraced the kind of white nationalism espoused by figures like Beam and Duke, while others fashioned themselves as simple patriots loyal only to the US Constitution.

In the 1990s, Roger Barnett founded Ranch Rescue, a group that he later claimed detained more than twelve thousand migrants over the course of a decade. Barnett had previously served as a deputy sheriff in Cochise County, Arizona, and his armed followers often wore garb similar to that of US Border Patrol.

Later on, Chris Simcox and his Minuteman movement represented a novel kind of border vigilantism that publicly distanced itself from white nationalism and racism while also policing the border for migrants and others who had crossed into the country. It's no surprise that proud white nationalists still found their way into the ranks of Minuteman outfits, which altogether boasted of hundreds of members, according to Simcox's own estimate. With the subsequent rise of self-described constitutional-patriot militia groups like the Oath Keepers and the Three Percenters, the Brookings Institute observed, "anti-migrant and other border patrol activities [became] not only a purpose in of itself, but also a training exercise for a much wider agenda, including challenging the existing U.S. constitutional order."[37]

By the time the first militiamen stepped foot in Arivaca and other nearby communities, the tradition had a long history to boast of. Of course, these militiamen had no legal authority to detain anyone, so many of the groups—take Tim Foley's Arizona Border Recon, for instance—began to claim that their primary focus was "observing" what was happening in the borderlands and passing the information onto the proper authorities. As you might expect, what actually happens in the desert carries the possibility of being far more nefarious than mere observation and intelligence gathering.

CHAPTER
THREE
THE KILLINGS

Ellen Dursema had seen Shawna Forde around town, in the grocery store and La Gitana, but she didn't pay her much mind. Why would she? Forde, a newcomer to town, struck her as odd, but Arivaca had always attracted unique types: those fed up with life in fast-moving, crowded cities; those seeking artistic inspiration in the mountainous desert; and those seeking to go unnoticed, whether by law enforcement or others. Dursema lived by a stubborn creed of tolerance—"Live and let live," she told me, echoing many of her fellow Arivacans when it came to their attitudes toward new people who moved to town—and Shawna Forde would not have been any different.

Although welcoming and friendly to newcomers and visitors alike, Dursema had always routed the bulk of her energy into the children at the Arivaca Community Center, where she worked as the director. One of her favorite students was Brisenia Flores, a bright nine-year-old whom Dursema recalled striking up friendships with the other children easily. Brisenia loved to pass her time in the local library. On the playground, she would let her playmates hold her by the ankles and make like a wheelbarrow.

Dursema knew Brisenia well, had taught her for years, and had worked alongside the girl's mother, Gina Gonzalez, at the community center.

One day in early May 2009, Dursema watched Brisenia in awe during an arts-and-crafts session. The children were preparing beaded earrings for their mothers—Mother's Day was coming up—and Brisenia went all-out. The child didn't believe that a single pair of earrings could fully convey her love for her mother, so she made some twenty pairs, using scissors and hot glue to slap together a cardboard stand for the jewelry.

In the weeks that followed, Dursema and the community center staff geared up for summer camp, where the children would pass the sweltering desert days with recreational activities, games, and outdoor time. When tragedy struck later that month, it was the earrings that Dursema thought back to. "She put so much love into that," she said.

———

Shawna Forde's journey to the US-Mexico border started in the Pacific Northwest and ended up with her languishing behind bars on Death Row.

By the time she touched down in Arivaca, Forde, a Washington native, had amassed an impressive rap sheet.[1] Before reaching adulthood, she had lived for years as an orphan and runaway. She racked up a slate of burglary, prostitution, and theft charges. One evening in October 1985, after engaging in sex work for two years in Seattle, the seventeen-year-old Forde—then known as Shawna Breitgham—made a miscalculation. She hopped in the car with an apparent john and let him drive her to a shadowy alleyway in Seattle. She placed his hand on her breasts, guiding it over them, and then took a handful of his crotch. Fifty dollars for a blowjob, she told him. "Seattle Police!" the man replied, whipping out his badge.

Her half-brother, Merrill Metzger, later recalled Forde teaching her daughter and son how to live on the fringes of society. "She taught them both how to shoplift," Metzger told the *Phoenix New Times*. Her son also later landed behind bars for burglary. "Shawna also used them to distract people while she shoplifted," Metzger added, explaining that she had once caught a charge for pocketing a carton of milk costing only three dollars and eighteen cents.[2]

Later, she worked as a music promoter, a youth counselor, and a beautician, among other professions—and she even tried her luck in local politics. Legal problems followed her wherever she went. She was convicted of assaulting the owner of a beauty salon where she worked around the same time she signed up for city council elections in her hometown, Everett, in 2007. Then forty years old, she ran on an anti-immigrant campaign—her half-brother later said she viewed immigrants as dirty criminals—and managed to pull in a surprising 5,892 votes. Still, Forde lost to the incumbent city councilor, Drew Nielsen, who garnered nearly twice as many votes as she had.

Not long after that, Forde took off for Arizona, where she joined a ragtag band of armed vigilantes. The group roamed the desert and hunted for migrants and asylum seekers, for anyone who had crossed the border. She first joined the Minuteman Civil Defense Corps (MCDC). That group had been founded by Chris Simcox, a longtime militia leader who later wound up serving nearly twenty years in prison for child sexual abuse.[3] Simcox and the MCDC boasted of being heavily armed, of using force to prevent migrants and refugees from irregularly crossing the border. Forde liked to call the shots, though, and tensions between her and the group's leadership led to deep divides. The MCDC expelled her the same year she joined. Still fired up about what she saw as an invasion of her country, Forde founded the Minutemen American Defense (MAD), a splinter group, and continued to prowl the desert in and around Arivaca.[4] She later claimed the group enjoyed thousands of followers, but former members revealed that membership, though always fluctuating, generally hovered around a little more than a dozen people.[5]

Under Forde's watch, MAD suffered from several problems—a lack of organization and ineffective leadership, for instance—but mostly the group struggled to pay for its equipment and weapons. Without a formal job, and hurting for cash, Forde did her best to solicit donations.[6] Still coming up short, she allied with local drug pushers in Arivaca and dreamed up daring plans to stick up their competition for quick cash and drugs to sell. Intending to funnel the stolen loot into MAD, Forde descended deeper into the very world of the dark forces she so often bragged of fighting.

When Jason Eugene Bush became Forde's second-in-command, the soil was tilled for bloodshed. A former Aryan Nations member and convicted felon, Bush had served time in prison.[7] Police also suspected he was behind a pair of racist killings in Washington, from where he hailed.

Forde and Bush teamed up with local drug dealers Albert Gaxiola—the nephew of Clara Godfrey, and a man with whom Forde had supposedly been entangled in a sexual relationship—and Oin Oakstar. Eager to eliminate one of their biggest competitors in the local drug market, Gaxiola and Oakstar provided the vigilantes with a name: Raul Flores, a twenty-nine-year-old independent drug dealer and Arivaca local, and nine-year-old Brisenia's father.[8]

In May 2009, Forde shipped off to Colorado, where she hoped to drum up support among other Minutemen. At a truck stop outside of Denver, she invited the men to join her in a heist, which, she claimed, would help her bulk up MAD's operations and eventually allow her to seal off large swaths of the US-Mexico border in Arizona. With the cash, she intended to purchase a forty-acre plot of land and establish a base for MAD's training and operations. Assuring the Minutemen that the operation would be smooth, Forde hastily drew a map detailing the general area in Arivaca that she planned to target. But lurking in the ranks of the Minutemen were two federal informants, Robert Copley and Ron Wedow.[9] Alarmed by Forde's scheme, they passed the map along to Chris Andersen, a Federal Bureau of Investigation (FBI) agent in Colorado. For reasons still unclear, Andersen destroyed the map. Only later would it be revealed that the drawing could have saved lives.[10]

———

Back in Arivaca on the morning of May 29, 2009, Dursema and the community-center staff were gearing up for summer camp. They planned recreation activities for the children, games and outdoor time to pass the sweltering desert days.

Brisenia was at home that morning when a Chevy Astro-van crept past her home on Mesquite Place. She stood in the front yard with her mother, Gina, who waved at the van as it twisted up dirt wraiths behind it.[11]

Inside the van, Bush, Forde, and Gaxiola scoped out the home. Someone waved back at Gina, although she didn't know then who the vehicle's occupants were. The van sped up, turned off the pothole-stricken road, and disappeared around the bend onto Hardscrabble Road.

———

Nightfall unraveled a shawl of darkness on the Arizona desert, covering the rolling hillocks, deeply carved valleys, and cacti-flecked desert prairies. Porch lights burned in front of the shadowed homes and double-wides scattered along Arivaca's back roads. On clear nights, the stars spangled the sky high above ominous silhouettes of mountaintops. Just beyond those mountaintops, smugglers were known to tell migrants that Phoenix awaited them, as well jobs and security and safety too. (Phoenix was actually some 175 miles away from Arivaca, which, according to some estimates, is a fifty-seven-hour walk.)

Shortly after midnight on May 30, 2009, Forde, Bush, and Gaxiola returned to the Flores's home on Mesquite Road, along with another individual whose identity remains unknown to this day. Gaxiola's business partner, Oin Oakstar, had pulled out at the last second; he claimed he drank too much and couldn't participate in the home invasion they'd already spent so much time planning, according to court records.[12][13] (In October 2014, Oakstar was found dead in a homeless encampment in Washington, "more than a thousand miles from Arivaca, his longtime home near the border," the journalist David Neiwert reported.)[14]

Gaxiola waited in the car while the others approached the home. They knocked, and the door swung open.

Brisenia's father, Raul Flores, appeared in the doorway, wearing only undershorts and looking sleepy. Forde, wearing a brunette wig over her bleached hair and identifying herself as a Border Patrol agent, threatened to shoot Flores if he didn't let them in. Border Patrol had encircled the property, she lied, and they needed to search the home as part of their hunt for a dangerous fugitive.

Flores wearily obliged. Dressed in camouflage, Bush and Forde stormed in. The militiamen scanned the room. Bush, wearing black face paint, stood by quietly as Forde ordered Raul to sit on the couch with his wife and daughter. Raul asked what was going on. "Don't take this personal[ly]," Bush responded, "but this bullet has your name on it."[15]

Flores lunged toward Bush and attempted to wrestle the gun away from him. Bush pulled the trigger, and Flores hit the floor. The gunman turned to Gonzalez and fired two bullets into her leg. Clinging onto life and sprawled out on the floor, Flores begged the home invaders to spare his wife and daughter's lives. Bush looked back at the desperate father and then emptied his gun into the man's body. Flores was dead.

Forde hollered to the pair waiting outside. The coast was clear, she assured them. She disappeared into the master bedroom, where she rummaged through drawers and pocketed a wedding ring and a few other items of jewelry. Bush questioned Brisenia, reloading his gun as the child broke down in tears. She was still begging for her life when Bush fired two shots off into her head. On the floor just a few feet away, Gonzalez played dead, first hearing her husband gasp, gurgle, and die, and then hearing the gunshots that killed her daughter.

When Forde returned from the bedroom, she warned the others that they needed to escape quickly. Someone was coming, she said. They smashed all the lights in the home and fled into the night.

———

Blood sprayed from the wound in Gonzalez's leg.[16] She scrambled to her telephone and rang 911. "Ma'am," she said, "someone just came in and shot my daughter and my husband."[17]

The Pima County Sheriff's Office emergency dispatcher, Tanya Remsburg, listened on the other end of the line, coaching Gonzalez as she typed in a flurry. Remsburg asked: Where had the child been shot?

"In the head," Gonzalez said. "In the head. Should I pick her up so she's not bleeding?"

As Remsburg instructed Gonzalez not to move the child, a sudden clamor of voices appeared in the background.[18] The dispatcher heard a muffled woman's voice. "They're coming back in!" Gonzalez screamed. "They're coming back in!"

Forde had shed her camouflage and pulled her back into a ponytail. She entered the house searching for a weapon they'd left behind during the abrupt escape, but then she saw Gonzalez still alive. Forde ran outside. She screamed, "Finish her off."

Bush rushed back in, and a minute-long staccato of gunshots sounded off. *Bang, bang, bang.* Gonzalez grabbed a firearm and fired back. She struck Bush before the home invaders again escaped. Gonzalez's voice returned to the line. "I think I'm shot in the leg. I'm not sure, ma'am," she managed to say, begging the dispatcher for help.

The dispatcher kept Gonzalez on the line until the police and the ambulance arrived at the Flores family home, having roared down Arivaca Road, around sharp turns and over sudden hills, from Green Valley, some twenty miles away. The police collected evidence and scoured the blood-spattered living room and master bedroom.

Later, Gaxiola returned to the scene of the crime, scoping the home from a safe distance. "Cops on the scene," he texted Forde.

"No worries," Forde replied. "All good, just relax, competition gone."

A few hours passed before Forde sent another text message, this time to her daughter. "Whatever goes down, I'm in deep now," she wrote. "I love you, make me proud, and do something good with your life."[19]

———

Back in Colorado, the Minutemen Robert Copley and Ron Wedow—the federal informants that had passed on Forde's map—called the FBI again. Forde had planned the murders, Copley and Wedow told the bureau.[20]

On June 11, 2009, police tracked down Bush in a hospital in Kingman, Arizona, near the small town of Meadview, where he resided. An eight-hour drive from Arivaca, Meadview sits on the Arizona side of the border with Nevada. Authorities arrested him in a hospital, where he had been receiving treatment for the gun wound he sustained after Gina Gonzalez returned fire and struck him in the leg. Once in custody, Bush admitted to both murders.[21]

The following day, a police vehicle pulled over Forde as she drove near Sierra Vista, Arizona. After cuffing her, officers dug through her car. They found Gina Gonzalez's ring in Forde's purse, as well as a belt buckle engraved with the letter G. Forde denied any involvement in the killings. That same day, police arrested Albert Gaxiola in Tucson.

As sheriff's deputies led Forde from the police house, a group of reporters jostled for a comment. Was she guilty? "No," she said. "I did not do it."[22]

Throughout the investigation, police investigators and prosecutors learned of the sordid pasts belonging to the three murderers. Bush's arrest led prosecutors in Washington state to charge him with the 1997 stabbing murder of Hector Lopez Partida based on DNA evidence, and the slaying of fellow white supremacist Jonathan Bumstead for "being a traitor to the [white] race and a Jew" that same year, according to court documents.[23]

Two years after the killings that shattered Arivaca, a court convicted all three for their roles in planning and executing the killings. Bush and Forde were sentenced to death, and Gaxiola was carted away to serve a life sentence. Authorities never succeeded in identifying the fourth individual. That same year, three years after Barack Obama became the first Black president, the nationwide militia movement reached 334 groups, according to the Southern Poverty Law Center.[24]

With her surviving daughter, who had been away at her grandmother's home on the night of the slayings, Gina Gonzalez moved away. Outside of the trial, she never spoke publicly about the night that cut her family in half. In May 2012, she filed a lawsuit against the federal government, alleging that the FBI could have saved Brisenia and Raul after the Minuteman informants gave them the map. The following year, a district court judge dismissed the complaint, arguing that the bureau was exempt from litigation because the FBI agent had deployed discretion in accordance with the bureau's policy.[25]

———

One January morning more than nine years after the killings, I met Ellen Dursema at the community center. We sat at a picnic table outside on an unseasonably warm morning. Behind her, a handful of Arivacans played pickleball on the tennis court. Beyond them, a large mural of Brisenia overlooked the pavement slab. Back during the first weeks following the murders, Dursema told me, she watched her neighbors and friends around town. Many were distraught. Some sobbed while talking about the incident. "People were devastated," she recalled. "The kids were terrified."

Children at the community center told her they feared going to sleep at night; what if armed men burst into their homes? "It was very tragic," she said. "We knew the family personally—we all did. And it was like, how could this happen in our peaceful, loving village? I know kids who could not sleep for a long, long time. I don't know if they still worry about it or not."

Even after nearly a decade passed, she often found herself remembering Brisenia as she watched the children under the mural of the slain child. "I don't know that they actually think about that being Brisenia, how she used to [play as] a human wheelbarrow on that very court."

After Tim Foley's Arizona Border Recon relocated to Arivaca in 2017 and attracted a slew of militiamen and vigilantes to the town—from Veterans on Patrol to the Utah Gun Exchange—Dursema still withheld judgment. Hoping to stick to her principles of being open-minded and not unfairly judging anyone, she resolved to wait and evaluate each individual on their own actions. Still, she couldn't help but understand the way her neighbors and friends responded to militias and vigilantes yet again targeting Arivaca. "I think a lot of those wounds are still open for the adults," she said. "I think as far as the militia goes, I feel like just knowing they're in town brings up everybody's worst fear again. Whether these people are that way or not—you know, whether they would do something to harm a family or a little kid—I don't know."

CHAPTER FOUR
EXPLOSIVES, DRUGS, AND CASH

Around 6:00 p.m. on March 30, 2011, Timothy Daniel Foley was wandering along the desert trails that unroll around Sasabe, Arizona, an eleven-resident town on the United States side of the border with Mexico, when he happened upon a group of Border Patrol agents.[1] He introduced himself, and the agents spotted a Glock holstered on his right hip.

A short, wiry man with leathery, sun-battered skin, Foley walked to his pickup and brought back a Saiga shotgun, a ten-round magazine, and a twenty-round drum magazine to show the border agents. He "appeared to support secure borders and the Border Patrol," one of the agents later noted in a report included in leaked emails, adding that Foley bragged about "concerned citizens" supposedly donating $350,000 for his paramilitary activities in the borderlands.[2]

Foley, who had recently founded Arizona Border Recon (AZBR), boasted of his "extensive" military experience and that of his followers, who were highly skilled in reconnaissance and sniper shooting, to name only a pair of tools in their supposed skill set. Foley planned to "conduct mercenary type operations" in Sasabe, Arizona, he said, and across the border in El Sásabe, Mexico. "Tim stated that he has Improvised Explosive Devices deployed in the desert near Sasabe," the report warned, adding that the Federal Bureau of Investigation was investigating Foley's claims to have laced the desert with bombs. "Agents are urged to take extreme caution while working in the area near Sasabe and should report any information related to this incident to their immediate chain of command."

Law enforcement from several agencies scoured the desert searching for Foley's supposed explosives, but they came up short. A bomb squad checked the run-down shack Foley was renting, but there, too, they found nothing. By early evening on April 1, the agents wrapped up their search. The whole thing was a hoax, they concluded. Agents watched Foley return to Sasabe that evening but declined to make contact with him, apparently at the request of the FBI.

Later that night, around 11:00 p.m., the agents spotted another man driving a white Chevy Impala with Arizona tags, not far from the Sasabe port of entry. When the agents confronted Todd Russell Hezlitt, a longtime figure in the local militia scene, he was carrying a weapon, wearing body armor, and exhibiting "erratic behavior," a report later noted.[3] Hezlitt, who had been interviewed by reporters alongside Shawna Forde only a few years prior, claimed he was searching for Foley with the intent to run him out of Sasabe. The agents observed him until he drove out of town shortly after 2:00 a.m.

There were no apparent consequences for Foley after state and federal authorities became aware of his armed outfit, a group that he founded in 2010 and still oversees as its field operations director today. The FBI investigated Foley, but in reply to my Freedom of Information Act (FOIA) requests nine years later, the bureau claimed to have no responsive documents regarding either Foley or AZBR. Despite his bombastic claims to have planted explosives, Foley somehow managed to continue operating without arrest, a puzzling pattern that continues until today. He carries assault rifles, gives migrants he detains the impression that he's a Border Patrol agent (according to former AZBR members who spoke to me on the condition of anonymity), dreams up scenarios in which he's wired the arid desert lands with explosives capable of tearing limbs from bodies, and carves out a trail of hate wherever he treads, but he's managed to evade the normally watchful eyes of law enforcement agencies both federal and local, time and again, over and over, for a decade.

More than eight years later, Foley has built a reputation among the militia community as a resident border expert, has fostered a media profile as a dedicated border patroller utilizing his supposedly vast military experience, and enjoys ties with several influential radical right-wing political figures. When Donald Trump barreled into the White House after the November 2016 elections, riling nearly half the nation into a fit of anti-immigrant panic, Foley and his ilk gained the closest thing they'd ever had to a seal of approval. But his paranoid crusade had started much earlier, during the Obama years, a time when militias surged and the tunnel-eyed focus of media outlets like Fox News and Breitbart narrowed in on what they perceived as the largest threat to national security: the border, a line in the earth that they considered porous and inviting, hardly guarded at all, and offering passage to anyone—from the dregs of ISIS to the poor peasantry of Central America.

Then a construction worker by trade, Foley started visiting the border in 2008, he told me during an interview in January 2019. After reading a call to action online, he joined Ranch Rescue, a militia led by veteran extremist Jack Foote. Foley told me that he lasted only three days. He continued to visit the border but eventually packed up and left Phoenix in 2011, moving to the borderlands and living in his pickup truck with his dog for several months. He cased what he insists were cartel hideouts, hilltops frequented by the human smugglers known as "coyotes," and the routes frequented by men—never women and children, the way he tells it—to cross into the United States. After a while, however, he hooked up with like-minded people—all fellow patriots, all enraged by what they saw as an excessively penetrable border—in Sasabe, and moved in with them. When the others moved out of town, Foley stayed behind, renting a raggedy shack that offered a clear view of the border.

Sasabe abuts the border and consists of a post office, a public school, a scatter of homes, and a single all-purpose shop. Many of the homes are abandoned and boarded-up, some of them having fallen into complete disarray: rotting wooden houses and sun-cracked adobe shacks that look almost primordial, as if they existed before the town itself and would, in one battered shape or another, continue to exist long after the last person packs up and leaves. The town's busiest spot, Sasabe Store, is a mustard adobe building with brick trim encasing the door and windows, and the shop attracts 95 percent of its business from south of the border. Signs fastened to the store advertise ice, cold drinks, gasoline, and fax services. Around back, the Hilltop Bar—an appendage of the Sasabe Store—serves spirits, cocktails, and beer after 3:00 p.m. on Fridays, Saturdays, and Sundays. The next closest watering hole north of the border is a half hour away in Arivaca. From the store, the border is a few-minute walk. Today, concertina wire adorns the wall that stretches for miles along the frontier, separating Sasabe from its Mexican counterpart. If you walk long enough, though, the fence simply ends, and the border returns to being nothing more than an invisible line, something dreamed up by men convinced that some neighbors could be fellow countrymen and that some, no matter how close their proximity, could not.

Around 165 crossings happen each day.[4] Border Patrol's green-and-white SUVs and pickup trucks rattle up and down the old road, the only one leading to town, coming to and from the crossing. Border Patrol agents often park behind brush, waiting to pull over passing cars and search for contraband. For some of Sasabe's residents, whose homes and land huddle up against the border, their closest neighbors live on the other side of the fence. They can wave at one another through the pipe fencing.

With less than a dozen residents, Sasabe can appear like a ghost town. Yet the desert englobing the blip of a community teems with life: mesquite trees dot the rock-studded plains; javelinas, rattlesnakes, bobcats, and foxes populate the land; drug mules and coyotes attempt to evade border agents; migrants and refugees either dodge authorities or simply sit and wait for to be picked up by them. At one point, authorities briefly closed a small slit of the Buenos Aires National Wildlife Refuge owing to "violent activity," but right-wing media claimed for several years onward that the entire park was closed to visitors.[5]

A stone's throw from the border stands the shack where Foley lived for around six years. He could hike into the desert in less than fifteen minutes, or post up on his porch and peer through binoculars into Mexico. From an operational standpoint, the budding vigilante couldn't have touched down in a better spot. Drugs crossed here. Money crossed here. Migrants crossed here. Sometimes, all three crossed together here. "One nice thing is that I was less than a quarter mile from the fence, and the access to the mountain only took me fifteen to twenty minutes," he said, "and then I was into the mountains where all the good stuff was happening. Location-wise, it was perfect."

When he wasn't on the trail of drug runners and migrants, Foley was posting screeds on Facebook. From behind his computer screen he railed against Barack Obama, whom he labeled a "jive ass, half-breed, illegal immigrant." In 2013, around the same time he admitted in one post that he had applied for benefits, he besmirched welfare recipients—"leaches," he dubbed them. The fatal mass shooting in Sandy Hook was a "false flag," and the 1992 Ruby Ridge incident, a deadly shootout between a white supremacist and federal agents, was a massacre of innocent civilians and a "government cover up." Muslims fighting the Syrian government halfway across the globe were "towel heads."

Accompanying a Reuters article describing a poll that found Americans supported deporting undocumented immigrants, he wrote: "The people have spoken. Deport all of them." Sharing a meme about the Department of Homeland Security warning that disgruntled military veterans could be vulnerable to right-wing extremism, he issued a threat: "Any questions on what the government thinks of us. They should be scared. Very scared." Along with an article describing garbage left behind in the desert, ostensibly by undocumented migrants making the dangerous journey to safety, he declared that "these turds will make the cities look like dumps." "This country is screwed up," he wrote, referring to an article alleging that the Democratic Party claimed to "own" the American government. "Time to get the pitchforks and torches."

Despite his public proclamations of support for Border Patrol, and his frequent boasting of cooperating with the agency, he often lambasted the Border Patrol as corrupt, referring in one post to "CBP bureaucratic dip shits" and the "ass clowns" making the decisions. Thanking an automobile body repairman for fixing his truck's damaged bumper, he appeared to insinuate in one Facebook status that he was prepared to run over people crossing the frontier: "We're now ready for ramming speed on the border."

Occasionally while on patrol, Foley stumbled upon undocumented immigrants or drug runners, reinforcing his view that AZBR filled a gap left behind by Border Patrol. Without fail, he would take to Facebook and boast of detaining migrants and "hunting" scouts before supposedly handing them over to Border Patrol. He often posted images to Facebook depicting individuals he and his posse claimed to have detained. In one video, he said he captured two cartel scouts and handed them over to Border Patrol agents. In another post, he said that he had caught an "illegal" and passed the person on to Border Patrol. Images on his Facebook showed him leaning through the window of Border Patrol vehicles, casually chatting with whoever was behind the wheel.

Nonetheless, Border Patrol denied any and all alleged collaboration with Foley or any other militia groups operating on the border. "Tucson Sector Border Patrol does not endorse private groups or organizations taking enforcement matters into their own hands," the agency told me by email. "Interference by civilians in law enforcement matters could have public safety and legal consequences for all parties involved. Border security operations are complex and require highly trained individuals with adequate resources to protect the country."

There, hemmed in by desert and in close proximity to the increasingly militarized border authorities, on the mountaintops and among the abandoned homes, Foley built his public persona as a rugged, self-fashioned soldier sacrificing the comforts of modern city life. A magnet for attention, he attracted militias and reporters from thousands of miles away. Often paying $200 a day, according to former militia members, to join AZBR's expeditions, journalists and photographers went out with Foley and his crew. He earned profiles in *The New York Times*,[6] *Wired*,[7] and *The Washington Post*,[8] and the now-shuttered *Al Jazeera America*,[9] among others, descended on Sasabe to profile the rising right-wing celebrity; a steady stream of anti-immigrant extremists, grifters, and vigilantes traveled from distant corners of the nation to see the border, witness the supposed national security crisis, and learn from Foley and his AZBR. A military veteran now patrolling the desert was a romantic story, but few seemed to dig beneath his claims: It was true, as Foley is glad to tell anyone with whom he speaks, that he served in the armed forces. But what he failed to mention was that some of his time in the military was spent in Fort Ord military prison, according to a little-noted revelation that emerged a few years ago on a blog, through an FOIA request for his military records.[10]

Even as militia groups around the country found themselves ensnared in federal investigations, Foley's stardom gradually swelled, reaching its pinnacle in 2015 with *Cartel Land*, an Academy Award–nominated documentary examining AZBR and a Mexican vigilante group battling the cartels on the other side of the border. In one scene, his men, all suited in fatigues, encircle a group of people that crossed into the United States. "If anybody touches me," Foley instructs, "drop 'em."[11] (Beyond its softball portrayal of Foley, that documentary later proved an unrivaled recruiting tool for the militia, former AZBR members told me.)

But Foley is not known for holding back his opinions or keeping a low profile, and it wasn't long before his relations with neighbors in Sasabe started to sour. His public persona swelled and he achieved relative fame, but the townspeople, having grown tired of his militia-like activities, forced him to sign an agreement barring him from lugging weapons and carrying out surveillance operations in town. One point of particular irritation, the document noted, was Foley's placement of trail cameras within the town. Locals did not want to be filmed, and they tired of camouflage-suited men, hungry for confrontation, toting rifles in their environs. He reluctantly signed the agreement and took down his trail cams, but the damage was done. It wasn't long before he began searching for a new border town to call his home, a new place to establish a new base. That town would end up being Arivaca, but the town planned to give him hell.

On May 29, 2015, some 250 militiamen and other right-wing demonstrators showed up outside the Islamic Community Center of Phoenix. Led by the organizer Jon Ritzheimer, many of the attendees wore T-shirts emblazoned with anti-Muslim slogans, waved American flags, and claimed that Muslims were stoking religious sedition in the United States. In post-9/11 America, the rally fit into a broader milieu of anti-Muslim hate, one encouraged and often financially backed by an impressively lucrative Islamophobia network consisting of anti-Muslim advocacy groups and well-funded demagogues.[12] Between 2008 and January 2017, during the years of the Obama administration, conspiracy theories postulating that the country's first Black president was a secret Muslim coincided with the proliferation of armed demonstrations outside mosques in places from Washington, DC, to Washington state.[13] Ritzheimer, like Foley, had spent years railing against immigrants, especially Muslims.

Although most of the attendees carried impressively intimidating weapons, Ritzheimer had organized security precautions: he'd called in the Arizona Special Operations Group, an armed outfit that shared at least one common affiliate with Tim Foley's Arizona Border Recon. Tensions ran high, and demonstrators gladly entered a shouting match with counter-protesters, but the day passed without incident.

The absence of violence, however, was uncommon for the Arizona Special Operations Group. Headed by Parris Frazier, the militia group was small, but it was highly active and covered ground around the southern Arizona desert. Although the group had descended on the US-Mexico border with the supposed intent of disrupting both cartel operations and migrant flows, Frazier had been overseeing a rip crew—a posse of armed men who stole drugs from runners and robbed migrants of their valuables—for months, according to a criminal complaint filed by FBI task officer John E. Kelly.[14]

On January 24, 2015, five months before the anti-Muslim rally in Phoenix, Customs and Border Protection (CBP) had pulled over Frazier in a routine traffic stop. The agents started casually chatting with him. Unknown to Frazier, the agents knew who he was. When they mentioned that an informal source that passed on tips on illegal activity had recently gone dark on them, Frazier expressed interest in contacting the source in order to better assist Border Patrol.

Two weeks later, on February 11, 2015, an undercover FBI agent calling himself Carlos phoned up Frazier. Carlos introduced himself as the informal CBP source and asked what sort of jobs Frazier was hoping to lock down. In Kelly's words, Frazier said he oversaw a "small group of Patriots he trusted, and they were trying to take care of (steal) anything that came up out of Mexico (drugs) or was going back into Mexico (bulk cash), but they preferred the cash loads going south."[15] In exchange for "decent intel" on cash moving southward, Frazier offered Carlos a cut. Law enforcement agencies did not have any of Frazier's men on their radar, he assured Carlos, himself oblivious to the fact that Carlos was recording the conversation.

On March 4, 2015, Carlos and Frazier met in person for the first time. Unbeknownst to Frazier, the conversation was again being recorded. Frazier laid out his terms. In exchange for GPS coordinates of cartel cash drops, he would hand over 25 percent of the stolen money to Carlos.

Frazier's men were willing, as the complaint put it, to kill "all of the individuals guarding the cash to ensure that his guys go home at night." After all, Frazier and his men could use the semiautomatic weapons they were likely to get off the dead cartel guards. More generous still, if Carlos wanted anyone else "taken out," wrote Kelly, Frazier said it would be no problem. All he asked for was a five-day notice because some of his men would be traveling from out of state. "If we have to dispatch [kill] some people, we will dispatch some people," he assured Carlos.

A few days later, on March 11, Carlos called Frazier, but Frazier asked him to call him on a new number attached to a burner phone. Carlos obliged, phoned the new number, and hit record on his audio device. From now on, Frazier said, they could speak only via the burner. Carlos said he may soon have a job for Frazier, but he needed to know if the militiaman had enough guys to handle it. Frazier said he had as many men as he needed. "It will be very violent and very quick," he continued, tacking on an ominous promise: the militia would not leave any witnesses.

On March 25, Carlos again rang Frazier on his burner phone, this time with concrete plans. The following week, Carlos said, he and his supposed cousin planned to drop off a vehicle carrying $20,000 in a remote patch of the desert. Carlos and his cousin had been instructed to leave the vehicle for money runners who would sack up the cash and transport it to Phoenix, but Carlos had a better idea. If Frazier and his militiamen could make off with the cash first, it would discredit his cousin, who, he said, worked for Carlos's cartel-employed uncle. With the cousin disgraced and out of the picture, Carlos would be able to supply Frazier with information for far bigger heists. Frazier was glad to help. All he needed were GPS coordinates, a description of the vehicle, and an exact time of the drop.

A week later, on April 2, Frazier and Randon Berg, an Iraq War veteran, suited up in camouflage, face masks, and tactical vests. They brought with them their AR-15 assault rifles, equipped with optical sights. In addition to planting $8,000 in the car, an FBI surveillance team had rigged the vehicle with video cameras and audio recorders. Frazier and Berg searched the vehicle, but neither could locate the cash. They left empty-handed. Later that evening, Frazier and Carlos connected via telephone. His cousin had pocketed $12,000, but there was $8,000 in the car, Carlos told him. Having failed to turn a profit on the operation, Frazier asked if any other jobs were coming up soon.

On April 9, Carlos called Frazier with another job. It looked like he was slowly trying to get his cousin out of the picture, Frazier observed. That was correct, Carlos said. "How about I lay an offer out on the table that we just get him out of the way for you," Frazier suggested. If the militiamen killed Carlos's cousin, Frazier added, they could "solidify" an "ongoing business venture" moving forward. Carlos inquired: Did Frazier want money for the hit?

"Yeah, we'll have to definitely get something monetarily out of it," said Frazier, adding, according to the complaint, that "it wouldn't be cheap, but it wouldn't be super expensive."

Sure, said Carlos, but why not carry out one more operation before killing the cousin?

Carlos had good news when he called Frazier on April 22. If Frazier could be awake and ready by 5:00 a.m. the following morning, there would be a car holding $20,000.

It would be parked at the Yucca Motel, a squat, single-story, salmon-colored budget spot in Gila Bend, Arizona. All right, Frazier told him: Call me back with the details.

Frazier cased the hotel and mapped the area, but Carlos phoned back with an update: The spot had changed; Border Patrol had been spotted in the area. It wasn't until the next day—the morning of the operation—that Carlos called back with the precise coordinates of the car. Frazier was worried, but not about the cartel retaliating. Law enforcement, he feared, might be observing. That didn't stop him, though. He and Randon Berg, his accomplice from the first operation, broke into the car. FBI and Phoenix Police Department agents watched from a distance as Frazier and Berg packed up the cash and took off.

There was only $7,300, Frazier told him on the phone after the operation.

Carlos explained that his cousin must have taken the rest. He'd have to sort this out, but now they could meet up and discuss the other thing, he said, referring to killing the cousin.

———

That conversation never took place, and Carlos and Frazier didn't catch up again until June 21, 2015, two months later.

Carlos had made the arrangements for the hit, but he hadn't been able to reach Frazier. When he finally tracked him down, Frazier said he had been out of town, working a job in the Midwest, and he'd forgotten to bring along his burner phone.

Carlos asked Frazier whether he was still up to working together.

Of course, Frazier said. In fact, he'd had the same question. He asked Carlos if there were any cash drops they could "jump up on," but Carlos said cash could prove too dangerous. The situation was too hot. Drugs, though, were an option, Carlos offered. They could be lifted and then flipped for cash.

It was a deal.

On June 28, the two men hammered out the details: Carlos knew of six to ten kilograms of cocaine that would be left unattended in a Phoenix warehouse. He could pay up to $15,000 a pop. Frazier asked for forty-five minutes to make sure his men were on board. When they next spoke, Frazier informed Carlos that the operation was a go, that his men had green-lighted it, and that they had scheduled a planning meeting for the following weekend.

Between that conversation and the operation, Carlos and Frazier spoke a few times by telephone. Carlos explained that the warehouse where the drop would be delivered was off I-10, but that he would have to give Frazier the precise coordinates later, as it could be one of a handful of spots they used for such deliveries. Carlos had buyers ready to purchase the blow, and Frazier prepared his men—longtime militiamen Erik Foster and Robert Deatherage—who were ready to go, wrote Kelly, "at the drop of a hat." The trio had experience in these sorts of heists, Frazier said, according to the complaint adding that each of them had "acquired a body count on different continents" and were prepared for a "firefight" if they encountered "heat." All the arrangements were in place.

After briefly meeting Carlos on the afternoon of July 22, 2015, Frazier drove a black Toyota Camry with no license plates to a warehouse off Thirty-Ninth Avenue in Phoenix. Frazier, Deatherage, and Foster cased the warehouse for fifteen minutes, but they failed to spot the FBI surveillance team who were hiding nearby, observing them.

The trio exited the Camry and approached the warehouse.

Frazier cut the lock on the gate. Deatherage acted as a lookout as Frazier and Foster walked into the warehouse and found the Hyundai Tucson housing the dope. The pair searched the vehicle and found ten kilograms bundled in red plastic wrap and secured with packing tape. Little did they know that only one of the packages contained authentic cocaine, while the other nine were fakes.

They grabbed six of the packages, including the one filled with real cocaine: A $90,000 haul, according to Frazier's agreement with Carlos. They put the contraband in a duffle bag and rushed back to the Camry, where Deatherage was waiting in the driver's seat. Frazier and Foster hopped in. Deatherage threw the car into drive and tore off.

That's when the plan fell apart. Blue and red lights appeared in the Camry's rearview mirror. Sirens wailed behind them. An FBI SWAT team was on their tail. As Deatherage sped away, Frazier hurled the duffle bag from the window as they reached an intersection at Forty-Third Avenue and Grand. All three of them were strapped with pistols and rifles. The agents briefly abandoned the pursuit, fearing that the high-speed chase could endanger the public, but a helicopter followed above.

As the militiamen neared Frazier's girlfriend's apartment, the surveillance team picked up the chase again, attempting to reroute the Camry into a parking garage on

East Anderson Avenue. They failed. The rip crew made it to the home of Frazier's girlfriend. Nevertheless, an FBI SWAT team quickly surrounded the residence. The agents called on the men to come out, and they exited the home with their hands up. After arresting all three and Frazier's girlfriend, they ripped through her home, confiscating rifles, handguns, assault weapons, and other items as evidence.

While in FBI custody later that day, Frazier waived his Miranda rights and admitted to carrying the weapons and ditching the stolen cocaine during the police chase. Nonetheless, all three later pled not guilty to the heavy felony charges thrown at them. The court set a trial date for November 3, 2015.

———

By the time Randon Berg became active in Southern Arizona, where he joined Tim Foley's AZBR and teamed up with Parris Frazier to steal what they believed was cartel drug money, he had served in Iraq and Afghanistan, racked up a felony conviction in Alaska, and been hit with charges for violating the legal prohibitions on a convicted felon, ostensibly for violating the terms of his probation.

He appeared in media profiles of AZBR regularly, often carrying a weapon and sporting a long, bushy beard.[16] Sitting in the back of a pickup truck cruising the desert, he was photographed rocking a camouflage boonie hat, matching fatigues, and thick camo gloves. A rifle rested on his lap. A resident of Sasabe remembers him living there with Foley for a period. A former AZBR member told me he was Foley's right-hand man, his second-in-command.

———

The trial of Parris Frazier got underway, and by February 2016, he was ready to plead guilty. In July that year, the court accepted the plea deal and sentenced him to eighty-four months in the Bureau of Prisons. Robert Deatherage, in exchange for his own plea, got five years. Erik Foster, in the end, got the lightest sentence: just two years with time served credited. He went home and had to report to a probation officer for the next four years.

For his part, Foster was only two years into his probation period when he requested that it be scrapped early. He hadn't broken any rules throughout that time, and his probation officer saw no reason to keep him under supervision. He had "complied with the rules and regulations of supervised release and is no longer in need of supervision," Officer Joshua Domschot wrote in a filing to the court. "It is accordingly recommended that Erik Stephen Foster be discharged from supervision."[17] In September 2019, US District Judge G. Murray Snow granted the request.

Shortly after Foster's probation ended early, Deatherage's sentence was also cut short. He was released on October 24, 2019. The longest-serving of the trio, Frazier, was set free in July 2021.

CHAPTER FIVE
IN TEXAS, A MANHUNT

Kevin Lyndel Massey was known to his friends and family as KC. In the summer of 2014, he left North Texas and headed down to the US-Mexico border.[1] Massey had a long history of seeking out confrontations, had been in trouble with the law more than a couple of times, and had big plans in southern Texas, where he wanted to establish a militia group and prevent the flow of migrants and refugees into his home state. Lean at six foot three, Massey, in many ways, looked like an average militiaman: he kept his head shaved, wore a goatee, and often sported camouflage fatigues. He gathered his weapons, rented a motel room, and prepared for a war against the people he saw as invaders.

Massey and his comrades founded the Rusty's Rangers militia, which sometimes went by Rusty's Regulators, on private land belonging to a sympathizer residing on the border in Brownsville, Texas.[2] Along with his fellow gun-toting vigilantes, Massey patrolled up and down the border, sometimes following supposed smuggling routes as far inland as Laredo, a city that sits three-and-a-half hours northwest of Brownsville. He posted videos of Rusty's Rangers carrying out operations on his YouTube channel, often racking up thousands of views, and made a name for himself in the media, granting interviews to American and foreign press outlets eager to pinpoint a flashy story about armed men exacting vigilante justice. Some of those videos showed Massey detaining migrants, slapping zip-ties on their hands and securing their arms behind their backs.[3] In others, the armed men intimidated migrants crossing the Rio Grande River, effectively pushing them back into Mexico.

Massey viewed himself as a "sovereign citizen," someone who could not be governed by federal law. The sovereign citizen movement traces back to Posse Comitatus, a far-right social movement that started to gain ground in the late 1960s and overlaps with the white supremacist Christian Identity movement.[4] Although loose-knit, the Posse Comitatus played a pivotal role in the growth of the militia movement in the 1990s. Its overwhelmingly white and Christian acolytes spread conspiracy theories, often with overtly anti-Semitic themes, and viewed themselves as the rightful historical heirs to the legacy of the Israelites. Their destiny, they believed, was enshrined in the Bible. The federal government could not impose laws or taxes on them, they argued, and many among their ranks opposed normalization with federal and state authorities to such an extent that they refused to obtain drivers licenses. By 2011, the Southern Poverty Law Center (SPLC)estimated that there were some hundred thousand sovereign citizens around the United States.[5] Most sovereign citizens preferred paper over guns—they would attempt to overwhelm authorities or prosecutors with paperwork, filing dozens, hundreds, or thousands of pages of documents in cases as frivolous as a dispute over a dog license—but some, like KC Massey, extended their ideology to the realm of firearms.

But Massey was far from the first to place his faith in the strength of bullets. In 1995, sovereign citizen Michael Hill drew a firearm on a police officer in Ohio—and was promptly shot dead.[6] In December 2003, members of the Bixby family, who lived in Abbeville, South Carolina—a town the SPLC believed could have had one of the largest populations of anti-government extremists in the nation[7]—took their beliefs to their logical extreme. The Bixbys, ensnared in a fairly typical and low-key land dispute, shot two law enforcement officers dead.

For his part, Massey brought much of the same anti-government hostility to Brownsville. While conducting patrols, he and his men would occasionally prompt the attention of Border Patrol agents. In a video Massey posted to YouTube in October 2014, he sits in an ATV while Border Patrol officers speak with him.[8] "You guys don't have authority on private property over us," he insists. He holds a cigarette, almost burned down to the filter, in his right hand. Blue and red lights blink in the night. "That's the law."

"Okay, so you're not going to listen to us," one officer says. "Is what you're telling us?"

"I'm trying to get out of here," Massey says. "Now hold on, this ain't about us complying. We are not under your authority."

"I'm aware of that," the Border Patrol agent replies.

"I'm *tryin'* to get out of here."

Another Border Patrol agent appears in the shot, and then explains that he appreciates Rusty's Rangers and their contribution to trying "to help out in this country." The confrontation ends with Border Patrol vehicles guiding Massey and whoever was with him—the person filming the incident—out of the desert patch where they had been stopped.

In another video, Massey films a line of buses some-where on a dirt road near the border. He pulls up next to a Border Patrol SUV and brakes. "Y'all still havin' a lot of the children comin' across the border now?" one of Massey's passengers asks an agent.[9]

The Border Patrol agent asks who they are, and whether they belong to a militia. "No," the passenger says. "We're just private citizens." Massey added a caption to the video: "Asshole Border Patrol."

In yet another video, Massey pulls his ATV up next to another Border Patrol vehicle. "The average citizen doesn't really know what's going on," the agent says.[10]

"Well, citizens right here are gettin' a picture," Massey says, pointing toward a cluster of homes in the distance, slurring his words heavily. "Because, you know, we're not out here tryin' to terrorize nobody, and we've made a dif-ference through here. These people, at night, they used to have to stay awake and the dogs barkin' all night."

The agent, whose face never enters the frame, complains that too few citizens cooperate with the agency: "They call themselves Americans, but they won't say shit. If you care about your country, you should fuckin' tell us, *Hey, there's a group [of migrants] that just passed here.*"

"I think we're givin' people a little more courage because they see that we're average citizens," Massey explains. "Because we're not paid, we're not cops, we're just citizens."

Massey could be friendly with Border Patrol, but not all of his exchanges with the agency ended on such warm terms. At times, his tendency toward confrontation reared its head.

Born in Chicago, Illinois, on July 2, 1966, Kevin Lyndel Massey spent most of his childhood and adult life in North Texas. At the age of two, his family moved to Dallas, Texas, where they lived in Pleasant Grove, a neighborhood in the southeastern part of the city. He first ran afoul of the law when he was still a teenager. He spent less than two months in the military before being discharged, and court records show that he later went on to act as a sergeant-at-arms with the notorious Cossacks motorcycle club, an FBI-designated criminal organization.[11]

In 1985, at only nineteen years old, he started to amass what would later prove to be a lengthy rap sheet.[12] That year, a police officer caught him and another man robbing a South Dallas home in broad daylight, taking off with pistols, a shotgun, and a handful of knives. Massey pleaded guilty to first-degree felony home burglary, and in exchange for coming clean, he dodged prison time and was instead sentenced to eight years of probation. Less than three years later, though, he was back in court. In January 1988, police caught him crawling out of the window at a Pleasant Grove home during a late-night robbery. He pleaded guilty again, but this time a judge threw him behind bars to serve out a five-year sentence.

After he was paroled in 1993, he married and had kids.[13] In the middle of the decade, he found himself wrapped up again in yet another legal battle. In November 1996, a *Dallas Observer* reporter visited Massey at his home and penned up a long profile about his addiction to flame wars in Internet chat forums.[14] Although he didn't speak to the reporter about immigration and the border, Massey was quick to show off his firearms. He already had plenty.

On August 29, 2014, Border Patrol agents pushed through the thickets of brush while pursuing a group of people they believed to be undocumented migrants. Massey was with John Foerster, whose long hair had earned him the nickname "Jesus," and together they had set out to patrol for border crossers. Massey carried a .45 pistol, a decision he made despite his prior felony convictions barring him from possessing firearms. Foerster was armed with a thirty-nine-millimeter pistol.[15]

Only a few days earlier, Massey had shown up at a campaign event for the Republican gubernatorial candidate Greg Abbott, who later became the Texas governor. He posed for a photo with Abbott, and later wrote on Facebook: "Trying to talk to Greg Abbott about the border problems. I gave him my number we will see if he calls."[16]

That day in the brush, his luck took a turn for the worse. When someone popped out of the bushes, Foerster raised his weapon, focused on the target, and prepared to shoot, according to court documents. On the other end of his gun was the Border Patrol agent Marcos Gonzales, who had been pursuing a group of undocumented migrants. When Foerster didn't comply with Gonzales's request to put down his gun, the court records revealed, the Border Patrol agent fired off four or five rounds, missing his target.[17]

Authorities later scoured Massey's room at a nearby Days Inn, where they found a rifle, three handguns, and thousands of rounds of ammunition. They also found what they believed to be bomb-making materials, including a container of ammonium nitrate, the same substance Timothy McVeigh had used in 1995 to rig the explosives that tore through a federal building in Oklahoma City, killed 168 people, and injured more than 600 others. Charged with and convicted of four counts of being a felon in possession of a firearm, he headed back to prison for a forty-one-month sentence. (For his role in the incident, Foerster was later convicted of a similar charge and sent to prison for nearly three years.)[18]

———

Massey may have been behind bars, but his imprisonment only fed his stardom. While he was locked up, many members of the militia community viewed him as a political prisoner who was persecuted for no reason other than his staunch patriotism. Throughout his imprisonment, he spoke regularly with the blogger Gary Hunt, who published documents related to Massey's arrest and trial as well as several dispatches that the imprisoned militiaman wrote from behind bars on his website, Outpost of Freedom. When I caught up with Hunt in late 2019, he was still in "indirect" contact with Massey, although the two men had never met in person. Massey was forced into "seclusion," he told me, despite being a "principled man" whose "word is good."

Long before Donald Trump became president by campaigning on the ideas of cracking down on immigration and building a barrier along the US-Mexico border, Massey "was basically as effective as the Trump border wall," Hunt told me. "The wall covers a much greater area, but it's passive; Massey was active. He barred Mexicans from passing a very easy crossing point, and he did the best he could to discourage illegal immigration. I back him a hundred percent."

Hunt had been involved in the militia movement since the 1990s. His first brush with the vigilantes came when he traveled to Waco, Texas, during the siege of the Branch Davidians compound, he told me. Led by the cult leader David Koresh, the religious sect was hunkered down in a compound known as the Mount Carmel Center, trying to fend off federal authorities who had showed up in late February 1993 hoping to raid the building and evict the cultists. Koresh's followers waged a gun battle against Bureau of Alcohol, Tobacco, Firearms and Explosives (ATF) agents. By the time the shots stopped, four ATF agents and six Branch Davidians had died. A fifty-one-day standoff ensued, while militia groups and other far-right outfits came out of the woodworks to support Koresh and his followers. (Timothy McVeigh, to name one attendee, had shown up, and the siege was later revealed to be one of the events that radicalized him.)[19] The standoff ended with a disastrous raid that sent the compound up in flames, killing seventy-nine Davidians, including Koresh and more than twenty children. For years, the event fueled the far right, and Gary Hunt was no exception. "I spent the next two years traveling the country talking to [people about] my experience in Waco," he said.

Like Massey, Hunt had his share of run-ins with federal authorities. In 2017, the FBI arrested Hunt for publishing the names of federal informants involved in the investigation of the forty-day occupation of Oregon's Malheur National Wildlife Refuge by militias and heavily armed vigilantes the year prior.[20] In the lead-up to the occupation, Hunt had participated in conference calls with Operation Mutual Defense (OMD), a network of militia groups that helped plan the takeover of the wildlife refuge. In those calls, some participants described Massey as a "political prisoner," a description that Hunt thought was apt.

In his prison writings, Massey often likened the federal government's prosecution of militias to Biblical times and railed against "tyranny" and the oppression of supposed patriots.[21] In a letter dated October 2, 2015, he accused the government of a cover-up, drumming up the wild-eyed conspiracy theory that his arrest was part of the "illegal and unlawful persecution of American Patriots."[22]

"My latest contribution to my country and state was to spend four months deployed to the Texas/Mexico border doing the job our Federal government refuses to do," Massey wrote in a blog post Hunt published on Outpost of Freedom. "I have personally helped turn back several hundred illegal invaders from various countries, while helping to serve the community of Brownsville."[23]

He urged others to "stand up" against an "evil" government hell-bent on stripping Americans of their weapons and liberties.[24] For Hunt, Massey's contributions were part of a broader pushback against a federal government that has "gone to the level of the Soviet Union under the communist regime."

———

It was July 23, 2019, the kind of sweltering day common in North Texas during the summer. US Marshals sat in a car down the street from the home they were watching as part of a surveillance operation. They had been searching for Massey for nearly three months after he violated his probation and went on the lam. On the surface, this investigation wasn't all that different from the ones that one of the deputy marshals, Keith Sieks, had conducted throughout his nearly two decades running down fugitives accused of crimes ranging from robbery to attempted murder, as he later told a courtroom, according to court records.[25]The agents interviewed Massey's relatives and acquaintances, and a lucky tip led them to Lone Oak, a town home to around six hundred people. Then their target stepped out of this home, the last one on Lakeview Drive, an old, weathered street littered with potholes and patches of unkempt grass encroaching on its edges.

The marshals took note of the pistol holstered to Massey's hip—by then convicted of multiple felonies, he wasn't legally permitted to carry a weapon. By the time he went on the lam in May earlier that year, he had been out of prison for less than a year. The US Marshals had good reason to believe that the fugitive knew he was being pursued. Shortly before a court issued his arrest warrant, Massey had failed a drug test, violating the terms of his supervised release. His probation officer's phone calls went unanswered, his voicemails ignored, and his letters unreturned.

Five years had passed since Massey gained infamy when he traveled to down to the border to hunt migrants and others crossing into the United States.[26]But throughout much of 2019, the militiaman, now fifty-three years old, was the one being hunted—the US Marshals Service, the FBI, and ATF were all hot on his trail.[27]

For several weeks leading up to that summer day in Lone Oak, Massey's Facebook posts offered clues as to his state of mind. He railed against the US government's "tyranny." He announced plans to keep a "low profile." He complained that the feds dragged him into a "battle" he never desired. "Fuck the feds and their probation," he wrote in one status, which was later included in a criminal complaint. "I am now a sought-after man, who is going to stand up and NEVER allow them to kidnap me again."[28][29]

The increasingly violent and paranoid nature of his social media posts led federal agents to consider Massey "armed and dangerous," Laura Dale, another deputy US marshal for the Northern District of Texas, told me in early December 2019. "These social media posts are still being investigated, and that's definitely something of concern," she said. "We're taking that very seriously."

According to court records, the squat blue-brick home on Lakeview Drive belonged to Massey's friend, James Russell Smith, who ran a tattoo shop down the road, and the marshals had been watching it all day. Massey came and went several times that day, the pistol always on his hip.

Around 8:30 p.m. that night, Sieks and other law enforcement officers approached Smith's home. "Everyone outside," they shouted through a loudspeaker. Smith and his wife stepped out, but Massey was nowhere to be found. "I can tell you a hundred percent he's not in the house," Smith told Sieks, according to court documents. "I don't know where he is."[30]

Smith allegedly confessed: When Massey showed up at his tattoo parlor four days earlier, the tattoo artist knew his friend was wanted. Because Massey was hungry and had nowhere else to go, Smith and his wife offered to put him up for a few nights. The couple let Massey use their phone, bought him cigarettes, and took him out for dinner.

During conversations that night and the following day, Smith and his wife told investigators that Massey had forgotten a backpack at their home. He had also left supplies in a storage container out back. Sieks checked both. In the backpack the deputy marshal found an AK-47 style pistol, he later testified, and in the storage container a cache of weapons.

The federal agents continued to search the neighborhood, but they came back empty-handed. In the end, they slapped Smith with federal conspiracy to conceal a person from arrest, a charge that carries a sentence of up to five years.

Massey, however, was still on the loose.

Since the 1990s, groups and individuals linked to the militia movement have built up an impressive reputation for armed confrontations with law enforcement agencies, and some of them have turned deadly. For that reason, coupled with Massey's own history of vigilantism, the ongoing manhunt could have morphed into "a situation that could quickly spiral out of control," Heidi Beirich, then director of the Southern Poverty Law Center's Intelligence Project, told me that December. "Massey's already been to jail, and had lots of ammo and weapons in the past, as well as bomb-making materials," she said, while Massey was still on the run. "He should be considered very dangerous and could react in a violent way if cornered."

With Massey on the run, Gary Hunt declined to rule out the possibility of a violent showdown between the militiaman and the federal government. I wanted to know if Massey would make good on his threats to fight authorities if they tracked him down. Hunt said the manhunt could always come to an end with bloodshed: "There's always that potential."

In the United States, vigilante border patrols like Massey's now-defunct outfit have deep roots. In the 1800s, rifle-toting militias patrolled the southern border to prevent formerly enslaved people from escaping to Mexico, and others later perused the borderlands to prevent Chinese immigrants from entering the country, as discussed in Chapter Three.[31]

In 1977, the Knights of the Ku Klux Klan headed to the southern frontier for a much-hyped patrol operation.[32] Throughout the 1980s, vigilant paramilitary groups popped up on the US-Mexico border from time to time.

A spate of armed standoffs and deadly shootouts—including the 1992 Ruby Ridge siege and the 1993 Branch Davidian raid—fueled the broader militia movement throughout the 1990s. A year after Timothy McVeigh bombed the Alfred P. Murrah Federal Building in 1995, killing at least 168 people, the militia movement hit what then marked a historical high at 858 groups.[33]

In 2012, anti-immigrant militias fell into the spotlight once again when J.T. Ready, founder of the Minuteman Civil Defense Corps, killed himself after committing a mass murder.[34] Ready, a former member of the neo-Nazi National Socialist Movement, shot dead his girlfriend, Lisa Mederos; her daughter, Amber; Amber's fiance, Jim Hiott; and Amber's baby, Lily. He then turned the gun on himself.

More recently, several people affiliated with border militias have found themselves entangled in high-profile prosecutions.

In August 2019, a federal court sentenced Joshua Pratchard, who had briefly been involved in the Arizona Border Recon vigilante group, to more than six years in federal prison on firearms charges. When authorities raided Pratchard's home in San Diego, California, they found a "firearms and ammunition factory" that included several unregistered weapons.[35]

Four months before that, the FBI arrested Larry Hopkins, leader of the United Constitutional Patriots (UCP), on federal charges of being a felon in possession of firearms and ammunition. The arrest came amid an uproar over UCP's detention of hundreds of migrants in the New Mexico desert. Court documents later revealed that the group had been training to assassinate several prominent liberals, among them Barack Obama, Hillary Clinton, and the Hungarian-American philanthropist George Soros.[36]

Meanwhile, Trump's frequent resorts to anti-immigrant rhetoric have energized the militia groups patrolling the southern border, experts say.[37] There were 216 active militia groups in 2018, according to the SPLC,[38] and many of them saw a call to arms in Trump's claims that so-called caravans of migrants and refugees heading to the United States constituted an invasion. As Trump escalated those claims during the campaign season leading up to the November 2018 midterm elections, militia groups from around the country packed up their guns and flocked to the border.

In December 2019, I spoke with Red (a pseudonym), who had volunteered with two border militia groups in Southern Arizona in recent years. Since leaving the movement, he worried that the situation would continue to get worse as the country's political climate grew more "extreme," with Trump's border wall fueling the rhetoric. "The thing with KC Massey, in the grand scheme of things, is that he was the calm one, at least compared to others," he told me, explaining that the leadership of most militia groups "would shoot every person who crosses that line, if they had their way."

Red had spent several years volunteering with border militias, including the Arizona-based Project Blue Light. He feared that more and more "extremists" would get involved in "shootouts . . . because they are trying to be somebody's hero."

He added, "They're all the same, and they're all extremists. I wish the government would actually do something about them . . . They're going to kill a bunch of people."

———

Two days after Massey slipped away from James Russell Smith's home in July, the local crime-stoppers group in Hunt County announced a $1,000 reward for information that led to his arrest, but his trail went cold.[39]

In October 2019, the A&E program *Live PD* broadcasted a short segment about Massey. "Kevin is considered an anti-government extremist known for his alarming rage," Robert Graziano, a sergeant in the Fugitive Apprehension Unit of the El Paso Sheriff's Office, said on the show. "We're asking the public, if you have any information on the whereabouts of Kevin, please come forward and notify authorities so we can get Kevin off the streets and back in jail where he belongs."[40]

But the militia movement and its supporters viewed him as a hero, someone who was being targeted because of his political beliefs. By late October, conspiracy theories cropped up on Facebook and Twitter, with some alleging that Massey's health had plummeted since he took to hiding in the woods—theories about his whereabouts that his most ardent supporters rejected as misinformation. Others began to worry that he may have died in the wilderness.

For militia supporters, the situation appeared dire. Melina MacInnis, founder of the pro-militia website Patriot Angel, was one of the administrators on a Facebook page created to support Massey. In October 2019, she called on followers to sign a petition calling for Massey to be pardoned. Due to legal obstacles, however, she was unable to send the petition to the president. Nonetheless, she insisted to me in December 2019 that Massey enjoyed widespread support, citing dozens of letters of support for a potential pardon petition and arguing that his manhunt demonstrated that the federal government will "hunt down people if they don't like them."

With several agencies searching for Massey, MacInnis warned: "The patriot movement and the militias, we're awake." Of the government, she said: "We see what they're doing. The founding fathers knew what they were doing. I think they're scared of us, so they're villainizing us, and they're using everything they can to turn any event back on us."

As unlikely as it seemed, Trump granting a pardon to someone like Massey was not altogether impossible. In July 2018, Trump granted full pardons to Dwight Hammond, Jr., and his son Steven Hammond, the Oregon cattle ranchers whose imprisonment on federal arson charges inspired the occupation of the Malheur National Wildlife Refuge in early 2016.[41] That occupation crested when federal agents gunned down LaVoy Finicum, who they claimed was reaching for a loaded gun in his pocket when they opened fire.

On December 11, MacInnis lost contact with Massey, a

development she feared was an omen of worse things to come. His health had been declining in recent months, she said, and illness sent his weight plummeting down to 150 pounds, down from the 200 listed on the wanted poster issued by the US Marshals Service. MacInnis feared the worst. "I'd like to think that he's still with us, but I don't know," she told me by telephone.

For their part, federal authorities planned to continue their search for Massey, no matter how long it took. "We are still looking for him anywhere in the country—and anywhere across the world," US Deputy Marshal Laura Dale insisted to me at the time.

Massey, however, had indicated that he wouldn't be apprehended without a fight. The administrators of his Facebook page said they were in frequent but indirect contact with him. On June 10, 2019, they posted an update they said summed up the fugitive's plans. "KC is NOT going to allow himself to be kidnapped again," the post read. "Death before dishonor!"

Two days after New Year's, the first reports emerged in a local newspaper, the *Herald Banner*, and then a death notice popped up on the website belonging to Lynch Funeral Service in Greenville, Texas: Massey had died on December 23. Confirming the news to *The Dallas Morning News*, Van Zandt County Sheriff Dale Corbett said officers found Massey after receiving a 911 call about an "unresponsive person" in a "small wooded area" in Wills Point, a rural community located a half hour from the Lone Oak home where Massey narrowly escaped arrest six months earlier.[42] When the funeral home later published an obituary, it described Massey as a "force of nature," a description neither his supporters nor his detractors would dispute.[43]

For the better part of a year, Massey had promised to take the fight to the US government, but in the end, he turned his gun on himself, dying of a "self-inflicted gunshot wound," according to the sheriff and the coroner.[44] After Massey's death became public, the US Marshals went silent, although I called and emailed them several times.

Whether Massey's death will prompt a response from the militia community remains unclear, but his legacy will endure as one of far-right vigilantism and anti-migrant militancy. With militias still flocking to the US-Mexico border, there is little telling how many Kevin Masseys might sprout up on the border. And if Massey never got the final shootout he had hoped for, there are plenty like him around the country, locked, loaded, and looking for a showdown with the US government.

CHAPTER SIX
THE BORDER CAME TO GET US

In the most dangerous pockets of the desert, Border Patrol, humanitarians, or hikers would often stumble upon evidence of the human life that had passed through. A tennis shoe. A doll. A campfire, sometimes still simmering. Sometimes they stumbled upon something more ominous, a testament to those who died while making the journey. A jagged chunk of vertebrae. A femur bone. A dusty, sun-whitened skull.

In 2000, fifty-eight-year-old Shura Wallin and her husband retired and moved to Green Valley, Arizona, an unincorporated retirement community located about a half hour's drive south of Tucson. Wallin had run a soup kitchen for the homeless and the poor in Berkeley, California, and when she moved to Arizona, she didn't have to think hard when presented with the opportunity to get involved in humanitarian work in the desert expanses swaddling the border. In July 2000, she started volunteering with Humane Borders, a nonprofit out of Tucson. A few years later, she joined No More Deaths, another organization that started in 2004 as a coalition of community and faith-based groups. In 2005, she cofounded Green Valley-Sahuarita Samaritans with a local pastor. During her first few years, she told me in January 2019, she and other humanitarians would find "an awful lot of people" stranded in the desert. Sometimes they'd find that their water jugs, which they'd left out for migrants, had been destroyed or dumped out.

While walking the arid trails, the humanitarian patrols lugged bags holding food, water, medicine, and first aid kits. Many of the stranded suffered from dehydration and hunger, and a bit of water and food could go a long way in the desert. Wallin often stuffed a pair of secondhand shoes in her bag—many of the migrants had walked for so long, and crossed over such rugged terrain, that their feet wore through the soles of their sneakers. Some had no shoes at all. Wallin washed their battered and bloodied feet, applied antiseptic solution, and bandaged them.

Wallin saw signs of death all around her—the bones and the crosses left in the spot where someone passed along the way—but it wasn't until 2006 that she walked right up to a dead body for the first time. She was shocked: somehow, the vultures had yet to feast on the man's carcass. She crouched down and examined his face. His head tilted back on the desert floor, blood crusted on his lips. His heart had failed. "It was quite traumatic," she remembered.

Wallin decided that she would track down his family. She found an identification card and learned that his name was Alfonso, and that he hailed from Guerrero, Mexico, more than 1,600 miles south. When she finally got on the phone with his son, a taxi driver in Los Angeles, she learned that Alfonso had lived and worked in Atlanta for eighteen years before returning to Mexico. Feeling a financial pinch, Alfonso headed north again, his son told Wallin. He crossed the border, and then the border killed him. He joined the ranks of the more than ten thousand people who have died crossing into the United States since 1994.[1]

Over the fifteen years following the founding of Green Valley-Sahuarita Samaritans, the group's ranks swelled to around 350 volunteers. Wallin, however, treated humanitarian action like a full-time job. In early 2019, at seventy-seven years old, she still participated in missions hiking throughout the desert. Several times a week she drove a deep-blue van full of supplies—clothes, food, and medicine—an hour away to Nogales, a Mexican border city located at the northern tip of the Sonoran Desert.

At the El Comedor shelter in Nogales, Wallin would speak with the queues of people waiting for a hot plate of food. Some of them waited to cross the border; others had already crossed and been returned.

When I first met Wallin in early 2019, she was as committed as ever, if not more than ever. Short, fit, and erupting with energy, she spoke with intense sympathy about the people she'd met in the borderlands. The children shook her somewhere deep in her heart most of all. When we first met at her squat, stucco home in Green Valley, we sat around her coffee table. She dropped a pile of crayon drawings on the table—children at El Comedor and elsewhere had given them to her. The artwork testified to the dangers migrants faced risking the journey. She lifted up a drawing of an SUV—green and white like Border Patrol's vehicles—chasing three stick figures, their arms raised in fright as they flee. Another, drawn in pen ink, depicted a group crouching under a tree. WE ARE HIDING UNDER A TREE, it read. In the background, a Border Patrol vehicle appeared to approach. WE WERE WALKING NEAR TUCSON, AND THEN THE BORDER CAME TO GET US.

Since 1994, long before Wallin moved to the desert, the United States had been implementing a policy known as "deterrence." In July of that year, a Border Patrol planning document spelled out a treacherous strategy for intimidating migrants and refugees into not passing over the border. By bulking up border security in easier-to-pass swaths of the desert, the agency could force migrants into "crossing through remote, uninhabited expanses of land and sea along the border" and "find[ing] themselves in mortal danger." The planning document predicted that "traffic will be deterred, or forced over more hostile terrain, less suited for crossing and more suited for enforcement."[2]

The strategy worked in a sense. In 2017, the United Nations observed that the number of attempted crossings had plummeted.[3] There was a dark side to the policy, one that was ingrained in the planning document's reference to "mortal danger": predictably, deaths continued to rise. The UN found that US authorities apprehended more than 340,000 migrants along the southern border—a 44 percent dip when compared to the previous year—while the number of deaths recorded by the International Organization for Migration increased from 398 to 412.

———

From the moment Donald Trump announced his presidential campaign in 2015, he vowed a severe crackdown on immigration, promised escalated deportations, and threatened to build a wall spanning the US-Mexico border.

Mexico, Trump said, would pay for the wall—a guarantee he would later ditch, along with many like it.

On July 11, 2015, the Republican hopeful took the stage at the Phoenix Convention Center in Arizona. Some fifteen thousand people in the audience welcomed him with rapturous applause. The business tycoon entered with his customary calmness, shaking hands with some in the audience. After greeting the crowd, a pulsating sea of mostly white faces and red hats, Trump turned to the issue that defined his presidential campaign and first term as president. He claimed that "the word is getting out that we have to stop illegal immigration; we have to."[4]

"We are going to make this country so great again. We are going to work so hard," Trump continued. Behind Trump a massive American flag was draped on the wall, next to Arizona's flag. He claimed that speakers at his last campaign stop had brought "hardened, veteran reporters" to tears. "People that I've known for a long time, that I don't even like—they're not good people," he said of the journalists.

A night earlier, Trump said, his friend Terry Lundgren of the Macy's department store chain had telephoned him shortly before his speech. "Donald, I had calls from Hispanic people saying they're gonna boycott Macy's," Trump recounted Lundgren saying: "I don't know what to do." Trump replied, "Terry, be tough. They'll be gone. One day! One day!"

Throughout the next sixteen months leading up to the November 2016 presidential vote, Trump continued to escalate his anti-immigrant rhetoric. He called migrants "rapists," "terrorists," and "criminals." His campaign courted the support of the resurgent white nationalist movement, and Trump failed to convincingly disavow the neo-Nazis and extremists lining up to ride his coattails. In August 2015, the former Klansman and rabid anti-Semite David Duke—whose Knights of the Ku Klux Klan (KKK) carried out anti-immigrant patrols on the US-Mexico border in the 1970s—announced that Trump constituted "the best of the lot" in the presidential elections, citing Trump's immigration policy proposals. "Trump is really— he's really going all out," Duke, a former Louisiana state legislator, said on his radio program. "He's saying what no other Republicans have said, few conservatives say. And he's also gone to the point where he says it's not just illegal immigration, it's legal immigration."[5]

Trump begrudgingly denounced Duke, but only after lashing out at CNN's Jake Tapper for bringing up the subject, in February 2016. A week later, Trump went on MSNBC's *Morning Joe* program and said, "David Duke is a bad person, who I disavowed on numerous occasions over the years." He added, "I disavowed him. I disavowed the KKK . . . Do you want me to do it again for the twelfth time? I disavowed him in the past, I disavow him now."[6]

Disavowal or not, the Trump campaign continued to breathe new life into the far-right movement, gaining broad support among the alt-right, a loosely knit coalition of white nationalists and neo-Nazis. Trump could condemn these groups all he wanted, but it did little to change the fact of the matter: they loved his immigration policy proposals and saw in them a positive step for advocates of a purely white ethnostate. Trump hinted at creating a database to track Muslim Americans, parroted wild-eyed conspiracy theories—the false assertion that Muslim Americans in New Jersey, for instance, had celebrated the attacks on September 11, 2001, which killed thousands—and proposed shutting down all Muslim immigration and travel to the country.

The Democratic Party saw Trump's hesitancy to distance himself from the radical right as a gift. Americans couldn't possibly vote for a man whose primary modus operandi was rooted in hate, could they? Time and again, public outrage over Trump's barefaced racism forced him to backtrack on his comments, but it never deterred him from issuing new bigoted statements. Throughout the 2016 election season, polls consistently placed Democratic nominee Hillary Clinton's chances of besting Trump between 70 and 99 percent.

On November 8, 2016, Americans around the nation headed to the ballot boxes to cast their votes. Even many Democrats—particularly those in more progressive flanks of the party—noted how much was at stake. A Clinton presidency might continue many of the worst immigration policies that marked Barack Obama's presidency, but Trump had promised an unprecedented escalation, a bonafide war on immigrants and people of color. The border was the adhesive holding together the loose-hanging, seemingly disparate pieces of Trump's political program. Why send troops abroad when they could be protecting the southern border? Why divert funds to social welfare programs when they could bankroll border security? Why give in to any of the political demands made by Democrats if they wouldn't accept Trump's border regime? For the president-elect, there entire nation existed insofar as its borders were ironclad, impenetrable.

After three months of traveling the country visiting some of the most marginalized communities—institutionally deprived *colonias* on Texas's southern border, homeless camps in Oregon, an impoverished indigenous reservation in South Dakota, and the poorest white-majority county in Kentucky's Appalachian region—I drove to a voting station in Forney, Texas. Waving a Trump flag—MAKE AMERICA GREAT AGAIN, it declared—seventy-two-year-old Ray Myers told me that Trump supporters weren't anti-immigration. A retired school administrator and a fervent supporter of the Tea Party, Myers said, "You just don't know who's coming across our border. You've got Mexican cartels and Syrians, and there's drug dealing and human trafficking."

Where we stood in Kaufman County sat around eight hours driving from the border, and I wondered how Myers could claim to know the situation for those living in border communities so intimately. "If you turn the country over to Hillary, you'll have a socialist country with government running everything from school to healthcare—everything," he added.

Suffering from severe strep throat, I went home and went to bed. Like most Americans, I felt fairly certain that the Democrats would dash Trump's hopes to become the next president. When I woke up shortly after midnight, however, the news looked dire. Clinton had beat Trump by a wide margin in the popular vote, but Trump had bested her in the electoral college. Donald J. Trump would be the forty-fifth president of the United States.

Less than two weeks later, the white nationalist Richard Spencer delivered a keynote speech at his National Policy Institute's annual conference in Washington, DC. Spencer claimed to have coined the term "alt-right"—a reference to the white supremacists, white nationalists, and neo-Nazis who would come to spill blood in the future—and he had

amassed a dedicated following of hard-line, far-right supporters, advocates of a purely white ethnostate. Addressing
the two hundred people in the audience, Spencer drove
home the implications of a Trump presidency. "America
was until this past generation a white country designed
for ourselves and our posterity," he said, prompting several
in the crowd to hurl their hands in the air with emphatic
Nazi salutes. "It is our creation, it is our inheritance, and it
belongs to us."[7]

"Hail Trump!" he bellowed. "Hail victory! Hail our people!"

———

After coming to office in January 2017, Trump made good
on his campaign promise to attack immigration. He slashed
the number of refugees permitted to resettle in the United
States, issued near-daily threats against migrants, and
tightened restrictions on both legal and unauthorized
immigration. During Trump's first year in office, his bel-
licosity sparked a diplomatic crisis between the United
States and Mexico.[8]

By the end of his first two years in office, Trump had further militarized the US border and bulked up Border Patrol
along the frontier. On April 4, 2018, the president ordered
the Department of Defense to send thousands of National
Guard troops to the border. Two days later, the Justice
Department directed federal prosecutors to clamp down
on immigration-related crimes. Between May and June of
that year, official data revealed that the US government
separated upward of 2,700 migrant children—although
the true number is believed to have exceeded that estimate
by thousands—from their families, whisking them away

to government custody. Facing massive public outrage, Trump halted the practice with an executive order issued on June 20, but his anti-immigrant program remained intact.

As the November 2018 midterm elections approached, Trump doubled down on immigration. A caravan of migrants and refugees—most of whom had fled Central America—was attempting to "invade" the country, Trump declared time and again.[9] Right-wing media went into a tailspin, repeating the "invasion" claim and drumming up fear over the supposed threat posed by a couple thousand desperate people fleeing political violence and economic devastation. Trump's rhetoric had predictable consequences.

———

Meanwhile, harrowing stories emerged from the migrant trail. As thousands of desperate people made the journey, most of them from Central America, those who spoke to reporters along the way described lives to which they couldn't return and expect to survive. They fled political chaos and gang violence, crushing poverty, and a spike in homicides, especially femicides, and armed conflict. For years, the so-called Northern Triangle—El Salvador, Guatemala, and Honduras—had been becoming more and more dangerous. In March 2018, the humanitarian watchdog the Washington Office on Latin America (WOLA) described "record levels of violence," near-total impunity for homicides, widespread extortion, and "lack of opportunity and poverty," among other hardships, in a fact sheet published at the time. "Being denied asylum or being deported can be a death sentence," it concluded.[10]

Daysi Peña, a grandmother from Honduras, joined one of the caravans that garnered international attention in the lead-up to the US midterm elections in 2018. By the time she reached Guatemala with three grandchildren in tow, she had escaped a plague of gang violence in her neighborhood back in Honduras's Chamelecón, which had one of the highest homicide rates on the planet. "I made the decision to join because there is no other alternative. I was overwhelmed by fear," she told the reporter Sandra Cuffe, who was on assignment for *Al Jazeera English*.[11]

Peña explained that a local gang had tried to recruit two of her grandchildren, both young boys, and had threatened her fourteen-year-old granddaughter. "One of them came over and told me she was going to be his and that if she was not his, she would not be anyone's. He would kill her," she told Cuffe. "It is not possible to argue with those people."

But safety was far from a guarantee for Peña and thousands of others like her who braved the caravan journey. Along the way, they faced the ever-present risk posed by organized gangs in countries from Guatemala to Mexico, and then, if they did reach the US border, crossing it successfully was becoming more difficult by the day as Trump's "zero tolerance" migration policy grew harsher and harsher.

Another person, Billy Martinez, was one of only two known individuals who had survived a brutal mass murder of migrants some eight years earlier. He had been traveling with a group of migrants toward the United States when they were abducted in Mexico, possibly by the Los Zetas drug cartel. The masked gunmen kidnapped dozens of migrants, drove them to a ranch, made them stand facing a wall, and opened fire. By the time the bullets stopped coming, at least seventy-two people had been murdered.

Back in Honduras, one of Martinez's sons was murdered in 2017, and he decided to make the same voyage that had nearly cost him his life just years before. "My first time was an experience of much sadness," Martinez told Cuffe. "Let's hope this time is better than the last."[12]

None of the risks on the migrant trail were new, of course. It had always been a dangerous—and potentially deadly—option, but so deep was the desperation to escape, so certain the feeling that staying was worse, that people continued to make the trek. In 2016, before Trump won the presidency, I had traveled to Austin, Texas, to meet a Honduran asylum seeker who had taken sanctuary in a local church. Hilda Ramirez, who was twenty-eight at the time, had fled Guatemala in 2014. She belonged to an Indigenous community in her home country, and due to the combination of violence within her family and from criminal organizations, she had made the more than two-thousand-mile journey. Once in the United States, the mother, along with her then eight-year-old son, Ivan, had spent eleven months in a US detention facility—more than a tenth of the amount of time the boy had been alive. "My son would cry and tell me 'Let's go home, mother,'" she told me. "He used to ask when we're leaving from there."[13]

At the time, Trump was campaigning on promises of mass deportations, building the border wall, and effectively sealing off the southern frontier altogether. But when immigration authorities targeted Ramirez and her son, the St. Andrew's Presbyterian Church offered them a place to stay, drawing on a long tradition of solidarity from faith groups that hoped to help those facing the prospect of deportation. Immigration and Customs Enforcement (ICE) generally didn't conduct raids on places of worship, along with a select few other locations, and the church could provide Ramirez and Ivan with protection. Ivan could leave freely, going to school and elsewhere, but Ramirez was unable to step foot off the church's property for eight months, until a court eventually issued a stay of deportation and, in effect, granted her more time in the country. "We didn't cross the desert. We didn't risk everything. We just simply opened our doors—and it's been wonderful," Jim Rigby, the pastor at St. Andrew's, told me. "Look at these beautiful people [Hilda and Ivan] Donald Trump has you afraid of. It's abject, craven fear—and it's pathetic."[14]

Two years into his presidency, Trump was still promoting the notion that people like Hilda Ramirez and her son constituted a threat to the nation. In fact, as the midterm vote inched closer, Trump turned the caravan into the "closing election argument" of the campaign trail. "If the migrant caravan didn't exist, President Donald Trump might have needed to invent it," the immigration reporter Dara Lind noted.[15] The president vowed to "defend" the border, even threatening to deploy the US military to the southern borderlands if necessary.

"Many Gang Members and some very bad people are mixed into the Caravan heading to our Southern Border," he wrote on Twitter in October 2019. "Please go back, you will not be admitted into the United States unless you go through the legal process. This is an invasion of our Country and our Military is waiting for you!"[16]

Around that same time, Sandra Cuffe went to Mexico and spoke to more individuals who had joined the caravan along the way. Among those she interviewed was Jairo Mauricio Ramirez, a sixteen-year-old orphan from Honduras. Both of his parents had died, and his uncle, with whom he had lived, had set off toward the United States months earlier. With no work, family, or education opportunities, Ramirez decided to make the perilous voyage north. "I always liked studying, but I could not afford to continue," he told Cuffe.[17] Contrary to Trump's claim that the caravan included "very bad people," the teenager hoped to become a doctor or an engineer.

———

Predictably, Trump's rhetoric took a toll. On October 27, 2018, the militant white nationalist Robert Bowers allegedly stormed the Tree of Life synagogue in Pittsburgh, Pennsylvania, and gunned down eleven Jewish worshippers.[18] As the media descended on Pittsburgh in the wake of the deadliest anti-Semitic massacre in the country's history, Bowers's posts on the Gab social media outlet—a popular platform for white nationalists and neo-Nazis banned from Twitter and Facebook—emerged. Bowers had posted numerous conspiracy theories alleging that Jews were behind immigration to the United States as part of a nefarious plot to undermine the country's white population. Shortly before storming the synagogue, Bowers claimed that HIAS—a Jewish nonprofit formerly known as the Hebrew Immigrant Aid Society—"likes to bring invaders in that kill our people."

He added, "I can't sit by and watch my people get slaughtered. Screw your optics, I'm going in."[19]

Trump condemned the massacre and visited survivors in Pittsburgh, but his campaign continued to amplify the baseless "invasion" claims. Fox News, the virulently right-wing news station that had become little more than a pro-Trump mouthpiece, hosted one caravan-obsessed guest after another, individuals deriding the caravan as chock-full of terrorists and diseases. Only two days after the bloodshed in Pittsburgh, the former ICE agent David Ward claimed that the caravan included "these individuals coming from all over the world that have some of the most extreme medical care in the world. And they're coming in with diseases such as small pox and leprosy and TB that are going to infect our people in the United States."[20]

Undeterred by the consequences, prominent Trump adherents, such as the far-right firebrand Ann Coulter and the journalist Sarah Carter, echoed Bowers, albeit in thinly veiled terms. Both claimed that the liberal billionaire philanthropist George Soros, a Jewish Holocaust survivor, was funding the caravan. Jack Posobiec, one of the original proponents of the Pizzagate conspiracy theory, alleged that Soros had rented RVs for the caravan's participants. The Republican congressman Matt Gaetz, a US representative from Florida, posted on Twitter a video that he insisted caught Soros employees dishing out cash to the migrants on the caravan. "Soros? US-backed NGOs? Time to investigate the source!" Gaetz wrote. Donald Trump, Jr., the president's son, retweeted the video.[21]

The swirl of anti-immigrant rhetoric, the false claims of diseased bodies flooding across the border, the proliferation of conspiracy theories—all together, the climate was poised for violence and repression, and not only migrants would be swept up in the wide net.

———

In January 2018, Border Patrol agents conducted surveillance on a site known as the Barn, in Ajo, Arizona. They spotted a pair of people they suspected to be lost immigrants, whom a federal indictment later said had come to the area after learning that they could receive water and food there. For nearly three days, the indictment alleged, Scott Warren, an Arizona State University instructor and humanitarian volunteer with No More Deaths, came to give the undocumented men food and water. On January 17, armed agents stormed the Barn and arrested Warren, whom prosecutors charged with providing to undocumented migrants "food, water, clean clothes, and a place to sleep."[22] A month later, a grand jury indicted Warren with two counts of harboring and one count of conspiracy. Altogether, the thirty-six-year-old humanitarian could have faced up to twenty years behind bars. The case was later dropped and Warren was acquitted, but humanitarians like Shura Wallin understood it as a warning nonetheless.[23]

Wallin had volunteered with No More Deaths in the past. The way she saw it, a crackdown on No More Deaths was a crackdown on the humanitarian movement at large, an effort to strike fear into the people who wanted to help those who had made the journey across the border.

CHAPTER SEVEN
VIGILANTES ON PATROL

On the sweltering morning of June 7, 2018, something bizarre caught Rachel Krause's eye when she sat down at her computer and started scrolling through her Facebook feed. Her friends, as she told me in August 2019, had all shared the same eerie story: a group of former veterans had found a baby's skull while patrolling a desolate stretch of desert not too far from Krause's home in Marana, Arizona. Curious, she clicked on one of the posts linking to the story.

Up came a video of a tall man in a baseball cap, with sunburned skin, red hair, and a matching beard. He wore army-like fatigues and sprinkled his talk with military lingo. Krause guessed he was in his early forties. Standing in the desert heat, the man droned on about his patrol group's need for supplies and support: Send gift cards, he appealed to his viewers. His name was Michael Lewis Arthur Meyer, the leader of Veterans on Patrol (VOP)—the same man who had accosted the bartender Megan Davern outside La Gitana in Arivaca.

He rambled for several minutes, and then rambled more. *This guy talks so much*, Krause thought. She fast-forwarded to the twenty-minute mark, and Meyer finally got to the skull. The "human remains," he said, reeked as if rotting. To Krause's eye, it appeared that the sun had long since bleached the skull, that the elements had taken a toll on it for some time. The Pima County Sheriff's Department wasn't responding to Meyer's calls, he said. Border Patrol was ignoring "human remains" north of the border.

Like most people, Krause didn't fit into either of the most common political clichés, liberal or conservative, though most of her politics skewed left of center. Friends and family would joke with Krause, calling her a snowflake—a description she both mocked and embraced, pointing during our first meeting to a cluster of snowflakes tattooed beneath her collarbone. Her husband served in the military, however, and she knew a bit about Border Patrol: the area where Meyer found the skull sits more than an hour's drive from the border, and that sort of complaint did not fall within Border Patrol's jurisdiction. She'd lived in Arizona for a long time, after all.

As the claims rolled off Meyer's tongue, anger washed over Krause. Sometimes migrants died in the desert—tragedies of which she was aware—but Meyer appeared to be up to something. This patch of the dust and sand also sat near the Santa Cruz River, and odd objects washed up in the area all the time. Once, during floods, a trampoline had even ended up in a tree in the nearby desert. From the way Meyer dressed—in military-esque garb replete with equipment, vests, and cargo pants—and the way he spoke, she was certain he'd never served in the armed forces. *He's just some clown in my desert*, she concluded, but she didn't want him spreading conspiracy theories in her area, either. "I just wanted him gone, away from my area, from my home, from the people in my community," she later recalled.

Deputies from the Pima County Sheriff's Department eventually arrived on the scene. They collected the skull and sent it to the Pima County Office of the Medical

Examiner's Forensic Science Center, where it was concluded that it belonged to an adult. That didn't stop Meyer, however, from spinning his story: It was a massive conspiracy to cover up child sex trafficking, he declared; it was a murder on American soil, he insisted.

Krause typed Meyer's name into a Google search, then moved on to Veterans on Patrol. What she found alarmed her. Only a few days prior, on May 31, Meyer and his followers had trespassed at the Cemex concrete plant off a frontage road near the intersection of I-19 and West Valencia Road. They'd stumbled upon a homeless camp on Cemex's property. It wasn't a normal homeless camp, Meyer insisted. The camp consisted of a hastily erected structure slapped together with logs, wood planks, and rain tarps. The scattered garbage—a vanity, a tossed-out car seat, an abandoned stroller, discarded children's clothing—told Meyer that it was a jerry-built dungeon for children being pushed into sexual slavery. "This is a prison cell," he said in a Facebook video, wearing an army-green vest as he climbed beneath the structure, "only kids are being held down here."[1]

Meyer furiously phoned local media outlets. On social media outlets like Twitter and Facebook, right-wing accounts shared Meyer's claims to the tune of thousands of times. Complimentary YouTube videos popped up: the local media outlets KOLD13 and ABC affiliate KGUN9 both broadcast Meyer's findings, taking a tour of the camp with Meyer and his fellow right-wing figure Craig Sawyer, who told KOLD 13 he had served in the military to prevent "things like this from happening here."[2]

Ducking down beneath a tarp, a KOLD13 reporter said, "It's when these vets came and found that area right there, that's when they thought something was suspicious." He went on to describe the vigilantes as "experts in the field of trafficking."[3] Standing beneath the scorching sun and speaking to the camera, Meyer flung an accusatory finger toward the city. "We're right there, and our city's right there, and our children are right there," he pleaded. "And 'it's not my problem if it's not in our backyard.' Well, now it's in our backyard."[4]

Neither KOLD13 nor KGUN9 confirmed these massive claims with the authorities. Had they obtained a comment from the Pima County Sheriff's Department or the Tucson Police Department, however, they'd have known that there was no credible evidence to support the claims Meyer and Sawyer had already sent spreading like a common cold across the Internet.[5] Within a week, Meyer's Facebook video had tallied up more than 650,000 views.[6]

Far-right websites flocked to the story. Gateway Pundit, known for propagating conspiracy theories, ran with Meyer's claims.[7] The narrative fit perfectly into myriad conspiracy theories that already existed on the Internet and off. On Twitter, far-right accounts claimed that Jewish philanthropist and billionaire George Soros, Democratic presidential candidate Hillary Clinton, and other shadowy, powerful figures lurked behind the cover-up. Even as far away as the United Kingdom, the tabloid *The Sun* ran a sinister piece claiming that a group of veterans—though Meyer, in fact, did not serve in the armed forces, Krause had learned—had uncovered a so-called "rape tree" at the abandoned camp. Straps on the tree, the conspiracy theorists told the British tabloid, held children in place while they were violated.[8]

Outraged by the police's apparent indifference to his claims, Meyer returned to the Cemex property in early July.

He stalked up a watchtower and vowed that he wouldn't come down until police dogs scoured the area for cadavers. Meyer climbed down later that night, and he was later arrested and charged with trespassing.[9]

———

In the days that followed the skull incident near her home, Krause pored over articles, social media posts, and YouTube videos. The deeper she dug, the more alarming behavior she found in the dark crevices of Meyer's past. She learned that only a couple of years earlier, in January 2016, Meyer and two other VOP members traveled to Harney County, Oregon, where they joined armed militia members illegally occupying the Malheur National Wildlife Refuge. Meyer and the others only left when a VOP member found himself on the losing end of a brawl with other militiamen, his face bloodied and eye blackened.[10]

Then Krause stumbled on an article about an incident in May 2015, when Meyer scaled an eighty-foot light pole in Surprise, Arizona, a thirty-thousand-person city near Phoenix. Perched atop the pole, he draped an upside-down American flag—a gesture used to signal distress—and demanded broad action to end veteran suicides. Meyer held his post on the light pole for four hours. Police and firefighters negotiated with Meyer, but he refused to come down. Events slated to be held at the fields were canceled or delayed. Meyer eventually relented, and authorities used a ladder truck to help him off the light-pole platform. Police officers slapped handcuffs on Meyer and medical examiners evaluated his mental state, concluding that he exhibited no clear signs of a mental health condition.

The officers carted him off to jail, where he was booked for criminal trespassing and disorderly conduct.[11]

In November 2015, Meyer landed a profile of VOP in *Arizona Daily Star*, a daily newspaper. Meyer and his followers showcased VOP's routine patrols in Tucson's Santa Rita Park, where they searched for narcotics and used syringes, clandestinely donned body cameras, waved upside-down American flags, and posted flyers issuing warnings to drug dealers and anyone caught engaging in violence. Meyer dubbed the patrols in Santa Rita Park "Operation Park Sweep," the *Daily Star* reported. "We're not out here trying to arrest anybody. We don't want anybody to go to jail," Meyer told the reporter, admitting, however, that VOP was willing to go "borderline vigilante" and detain someone, if necessary.[12]

VOP provided homeless veterans and women in the park with free food, security, and a campfire for warmth at night. Nonveteran men were permitted to stay for three days, but after that, they were expected to chop firewood, help clean up the campsite, or carry out other tasks in exchange for VOP's services. Local police coordinated with VOP and enjoyed a "good working relationship" with the group, Sergeant Pete Dugan told the *Daily Star*.

Not everyone sleeping in Santa Rita Park approved of the VOP. A homeless man who frequented the area and, accused Meyer's group of "trying to be law enforcement" and issuing threats each evening around nightfall. "They just need to go," he told the newspaper. "They're vigilantes."

In 2014, Krause learned, Meyer had traveled to Nevada, where hundreds of militiamen and vigilantes had gathered to support the radical right-wing rancher Cliven Bundy and his family during an armed standoff with agents from the Bureau of Land Management (BLM). The armed standoff resulted in the BLM officers releasing Bundy's cattle, which the agents had previously confiscated, and it served as a rallying cry for militia groups and adherents of the patriot movement. Describing himself as an organizer for the Three Percenters militia group, Meyer mingled with like-minded vigilantes there. Yet he quickly ran afoul of the others after he phoned the police. By the time the dust settled, Meyer had earned a poor reputation and a nickname, "Screwy Louie," that continued to follow him wherever he went.

Krause wondered: *Who is this guy?* She thought back to the Pizzagate conspiracy theory, which claimed that high-ranking Democrats had been involved in a child sex ring hosted by the Comet Ping Pong pizza parlor in Washington, DC. That whirlwind of misinformation, pushed by far-right websites like InfoWars and Your News Wire, had prompted a man to open fire on the restaurant a month after Donald Trump won the US presidential elections. *Could Meyer prompt similar vigilante violence here?*

———

A few days later, Krause created a Facebook page that landed her in Meyer's sights. "Citizens Against VOP," she called it. Each day, the forty-two-year-old stay-at-home mother would scour the vigilante group's social media pages.

She dove further into her research, but beyond charges, Meyer's personal past proved elusive. Born in 1978, Meyer left a trail of public records that stretched back to Ohio and North Carolina. He had racked up a slew of misdemeanor charges in several states back east, and at least one felony conviction: assault, breaking and entering, assault with bodily fluid (ostensibly by spitting on someone), criminal littering on public land, criminal mischief, illegal processing of drug documents. The felony conviction, Krause reasoned, explained why he never carried a weapon in his videos, although many of the men and women around him packed firearms.

Through her new Facebook page, Krause tracked down people who knew Meyer: former VOP members, militiamen who had been at the Bundy Ranch in Nevada, and military-veteran advocates who'd crossed paths with him. She met people in spots like McDonald's and Denny's. She accumulated all the information she could, saving it on Google Drive, and forming a clearer picture of who Meyer was. Everything she found confirmed her suspicions of him: dangerous and prone to violence.

On Twitter and Facebook, Krause posted screenshots of Meyer's comments—often screeds that hinted at violence—from his own accounts and from accounts linked to VOP. Meyer didn't like criticism of his group, however, and he had a penchant for lashing out at his opponents. He uniformly deemed his opponents pedophiles and drug addicts, accusing them of complicity in the child sex trafficking rings he dreamed up all around him.

In late July 2018, Meyer noticed Krause, and he struck back. On one of his VOP accounts—he ran many at the time because he often lost pages to Twitter and Facebook suspensions—he shot out a signal to his followers and supporters: Rachel Krause, he said, was involved in the very type of criminal activity he had been exposing. In that post, he broadcast her address for everyone to see.

Sixty-nine-year-old Terry Sayles, who had driven down to Arivaca to sound the alarm on Meyer earlier that year, sat in the back of the gallery and observed Michael Lewis Arthur Meyer during a court hearing one day in October 2018. He looked around the courtroom, noted the empty seats, and, as he told me in August 2019, realized he was the only observer that day. *Meyer looks agitated*, he thought. He wondered if Meyer recognized him, but he felt fairly certain he hadn't.

After the hearing concluded, as the vigilante and his wife made their way out of the courtroom, the wife nodded in Sayles's direction. "What about him?" she asked within earshot of Sayles.

"I'll do him outside," Meyer told her, according to Sayles's recollection.

Sayles, a retired school teacher from northeastern Washington, had moved to Arizona a couple of years prior. A self-started sleuth, he'd tracked militias, vigilantes, and far-right extremists back in Washington and here in Arizona. He'd been keeping an eye on Meyer since June, around the time that the VOP leader drummed up the Cemex conspiracy theory. As those conspiracy theories swelled online, Sayles tracked down the homeless people that had lived at the camp and tried to connect them with the journalists to dispel the lies. Since then, he'd come to the courthouse for a handful of Meyer's frequent hearings.

The judge asked Sayles if he needed security guards to accompany him to the car, but he declined. When he stepped out of the courthouse, Meyer stood there waiting for him, dressed in a T-shirt emblazoned with the word

QANON: the name of a popular far-right conspiracy theory that alleged a deep-state plot to oust Trump and persecute the president's followers. Although QAnon began in fringe corners of the Internet, it quickly spread to pro-Trump rallies, where some participants held banners and placards signaling their fear of the supposed coup plan.

Sayles looked up at a red-faced Meyer. "You get to see what you wanted to see in court?" Meyer asked. "I'm still here, still standin', ain't I, you piece of shit? You fuckin' piece-of-shit coward."

"You are a horse's ass," Sayles said. He knew that Meyer was capable of violence, and recalled an incident in which the vigilante had allegedly emptied a can of pepper spray on a homeless man in Tucson some months back. *A bully,* Sayles thought. *He needs to know I won't back down. I'm right here, if you want a piece of me, and I won't back down.* He repeated: "You are a horse's ass." A ball cap adorned his head and he wore sunglasses, but Meyer zoomed in his camera phone onto Sayles's face. Sayles turned and started to walk away.

"Over fifty kids rescued," Meyer yelled, "and your piece-of-shit ass is trying to stop us."

Sayles spun back around. He opened his arms wide. "Who have you rescued, Lewis?"

"Over fifty kids. Go look at the videos."

"Border Patrol was there."

"No," Meyer retorted. "We were there before Border Patrol, you piece of shit. What's your name? Tell everybody your name. Be proud of who you are."

"Terry Sayles. S-a-y-l-e-s." He turned again to walk off, but Meyer pursued him, the camera still rolling.

"This is the piece of shit who likes to come to our

courthouse," Meyer told his live stream, "and likes to stalk me and my wife. This piece-of-shit motherfucker right here."

Sayles swung his body around. Stalking? Sure, I've come to court hearings, he thought, but I don't even know where the guy lives. I've probably never been within twenty miles of his home. "What? What?" Sayles demanded. He stood in place as Meyer inched toward him. "What? What?"

"You're a piece of shit, motherfucker," Meyer repeated several times.

Sayles shoved Meyer away. "You can move up on me all you like," Meyer said. "You're a piece-of-shit motherfucker. Back off me. I'll lay your fuckin' ass out. I will. Don't touch me again. I'll defend myself."

They exchanged more words, and Sayles tried again to walk off. Meyer followed him, screaming and accusing him of stalking. "You guys see this piece of shit?" Meyer yelled into his phone. "This guy, this guy is the one trying to stop us from rescuing kids in the desert."

Sayles walked on and tried to ignore him. I'll be doxxed for this, he thought. I'm going to catch crap, but at my age, so what? Have at it. I'm done not standing up for what's right.

As Sayles finally reached the intersection and waited to cross, Meyer ended the confrontation with a harrowing threat: "I'm going to start following your family, if you don't stop following mine."

———

One morning in March 2018, a pickup truck rattled to a halt in front of Humane Borders, a nonprofit group based in Tucson. Joel Smith, the aid organization's manager of operations, greeted the driver when he entered the office. As Smith told me when I interviewed him in January 2019, he had grown up split between Arizona and Europe—his father served in the US Navy—but he'd been back in Tucson as a full-time resident for years, and he'd worked at Humane Borders since 2009. Because the group works in many of the most perilous swaths of the desert, where volunteers put out food and water for migrants and refugees making the journey, Smith often encountered new people interested in sparing free time to help out. Although this man appeared a little older than most potential volunteers, he introduced himself to Smith as a student at Pima Community College who was from Montana. He told Smith he was eager to learn more about Humane Borders's work. The man, standing more than six feet tall and with red hair, struck Smith as a bit strange, but Arizona had always attracted odd types. After the man left, Smith didn't give him much thought. He didn't hear back from him, but humanitarian work is self-less and difficult, and many people that expressed interest in volunteering later failed to follow up.

Over the next few months, however, Smith's water drops started ending up destroyed. He would show up at a spot in the desert to check on the large blue water tanks filled by him and his volunteers, only to find that they had been stabbed with knives and left to drain out onto the arid ground. Smith wondered who had destroyed the water tanks. Although Border Patrol agents had been known to destroy them in the past, hoping to deter migrants from entering the country, Smith had reached an agreement with them not to damage his water stations. Sometime in the summer of 2018, though, videos started popping up on

Facebook and Twitter: Michael Lewis Arthur Meyer and his supporters were bragging about destroying the water tanks, and Meyer was the same man who had shown up at Smith's office only a few months earlier, he suspected. "Usually we get people vandalizing them and we have no idea who did it," Smith recalled, "but he is putting it on fucking YouTube."

Smith started keeping tabs on Meyer and the VOP. He saved the videos of Meyer destroying the water stations. *Evidence*, he thought. While bouncing across the desert to check on water stations, he never saw Meyer—or any other vigilantes—although he often found water tanks sliced open, their contents leaked out onto the ragged earth.

Then Smith heard that Meyer had a court hearing in Tucson on November 2, 2018. He drove over to the courthouse and took a seat in the back of the room. Smith made eye contact with Meyer, and Meyer flashed a grimace his way. Smith stayed quiet, listening with interest. When the hearing concluded, he stepped out into the sunlight. Standing there with a reddened face and puffed chest, wearing an olive-green T-shirt, faded blue cargo pants, and hiking boots, was Meyer. "You're staging humanitarian aid for child traffickers . . . and you're gonna try and jump on me in court," Meyer said, throwing his arms around wildly. "Who the fuck do you think you are, buddy?"

Smith maintained his calm and shoved his hands in his pockets. "I came to talk to you," he replied, refusing to raise his voice.

"No," Meyer shot back. "You didn't come to talk to me. You came to run your fuckin' mouth."

Meyer launched into a profanity-laced tirade, accusing

Smith again and again of helping child traffickers. "What about the bad guys?" Meyer demanded. He shoved his finger toward Smith several times as he spoke. "What about the ones dragging children who were unaccompanied? What about the drugs? What do we do to stop them from coming? You put up aid, and you let *everyone* come."

"No—" Smith began.

"That's bullshit, man," Meyer shouted.

"I prevent deaths," Smith shot back.

"You didn't prevent deaths. You know who prevented deaths? Veterans on Patrol. Two weeks ago, ninety-four Guatemalans, four dozen kids . . . they didn't even have a gallon of water per person, and they thought they had to cross a mountain to get to Phoenix. They wouldn't even have made it [survived]—three of those children ended up in the hospital—they wouldn't have made it to that mountain, they wouldn't have made it to your water station."

"So that's why you guys attacked it [the water station]?"

"We didn't attack it. I'm gonna go driving around on the border with a blue flag, so they come running up to us and they know that your blue flags feed poison. I'm gonna make sure they know they can't trust your blue flags because they're gonna get caught every time they [approach them] because we don't aid child traffickers."

Smith told Meyer he came to the courthouse to open a dialogue.

"I don't listen to the devil," Meyer shot back.

Tensing his muscles, Smith closed the space between the two. He clenched his fists, but Meyer didn't move back. "I know you," Meyer screamed. "You go and fucking put water for child traffickers. So, I mean, I know your job. What's my job? My job is to stop you from your job because you're aiding child traffickers. And I don't give a shit what permit they give you, fuckface. They're dragging children."

"Fuckface?" Smith shouted back. "Fuckface?"

Smith sucked in a deep breath, held it in his chest, and moved yet closer to Meyer, who extended an arm and kept Smith at bay. Smith nodded his head as if begging Meyer to strike him.

"Please step away," a woman shouted from behind the phone recording the incident.

A police officer exited the courthouse. "Are we okay?" the officer asked, lifting his walkie-talkie to call for backup.

"Yes, sir, I'm leaving the scene, sir," Meyer responded, and both men walked off.

———

In the weeks following Meyer's verbal assault on Joel Smith, VOP's social media accounts upped the ante, declaring war on "criminals" the group claimed supported open borders. In Meyer's mind, like in the minds of all conspiracy theorists, the supposedly evil plots in motion could never be disproved: any evidence offered was in and of itself part of the cover-up, a product of the shadowy forces acting behind the scenes, far from the public eye, somewhere in a boardroom where people undoubtedly plotted the sinister strategies for dismantling America and replacing its occupants. How genuinely those beliefs were held by the people weaponizing them, and how much of their paranoid *Weltanschauung* was contrived to attract support and money, was rarely clear, but that particular arithmetic mattered less when considering the impact. Conspiracy theories could lead to bloodshed, could prompt someone to pick up a gun and enact vigilante justice, and could ruin lives and livelihoods.

Drawing from the age-old anti-Semitic conspiracy theory that places Jews behind immigration from the Global South to Western countries, the @VOPreal Twitter account painted a grim picture: a powerful elite including George Soros, the Clintons, the Rothschild family, and Joel Smith himself operated human smuggling routes that provided passage for supposed Mexican cartel businesses profiting from funneling children into sexual slavery.

On November 24, 2018, the VOP Twitter account posted: "American Patriots in . . . VOP . . . are now at War with the Open Border criminals in Pima County." The tweet went on to mention Tucson mayor Jonathan Rothschild, County Attorney Barbara LaWall, Humane Borders operations manager Joel Smith, Tucson police chief Christopher Magnus, County Sheriff Mark Napier, US Representative Raúl Grijalva, the humanitarian aid group No More Deaths, and "that POS George Soros."

———

Hoping to uncover yet more dirt on Screwy Louie, Krause began tracking down former VOP members through social media, mostly via Facebook. Well-educated and committed to a topic when she took interest, she scoured public records, anonymous blogs deriding VOP, and news articles making passing references to the group and its firebrand leader. She filled the empty slots of her day with research, phone calls with people who'd crossed Meyer's path, and discreet meetings with rugged militiamen and desert vigilantes in McDonald's booths.

Her biggest break came when she got Jeff Kagan, a young Texan who'd traveled to the Oregon militia occupation with Meyer, on the phone. She said Kagan alerted her to what he described as a mysterious death at a VOP camp in Maricopa County, the county that houses Phoenix and that voted in Joe Arpaio, the infamous far-right sheriff known for exacting a slew of inhuman policies targeting migrants and incarcerated people, six times.

———

On the morning of December 10, 2018, Rachel Krause was washing dishes after preparing lunch for her eleven-year-old daughter when her dogs suddenly started barking in a fury. *Maybe the postman arrived,* she thought. Then she heard a burst of commotion from the front yard. Someone screamed. *Did someone just shout my name?*

She walked to the front door, opened it, and looked out. A man stood there on the street in front of her home, shouting and throwing his arms around in a tangle. She didn't have her glasses on, and it took her a moment to realize who had just showed up at her family home.

"Let's be clear, this is Lewis Arthur outside Rachel Krause's house," Meyer shouted. He livestreamed the incident on his phone. "Let every neighbor out here know that this piece of shit, Luciferian piece of shit, is aiding child traffickers."

Krause's heart thrashed in her chest. She'd always suspected that Meyer might show up one day, but that didn't lessen the shock. *He really crossed this line,* she thought.

"Now she just poked her head outside . . . but I am on a public road, as you can see," Meyer said. "Rachel Krause is aiding child traffickers. Here she comes."

Krause slammed the door. She ran back to the kitchen and whisked her daughter off to the computer room. She told the girl to eat her lunch in there and play computer games. She grabbed her phone and her pistol, a gray nine-millimeter Sig Sauer.

"She is a fucking coward, piece of shit, and here I stand on public road to show you what this piece of shit is doing," Meyer continued. "Here she is: she can't hide behind her computer no more, America. She can't hide behind her computer no more, America."

She swung the front door open and toed out into the barren, rock-studded lawn. A sudden calm coursed through her. *I have to protect my daughter,* she told herself. She held the pistol awkwardly at her side, almost childlike. She dialed 911 and placed the phone to her ear. Under a gunmetal sky, she sat on the hard earth. She held the phone to her head. Her finger remained on the trigger guard. Worried that he brought backup—*Is one of his henchmen waiting around the corner?* she asked herself—she addressed him for the first time: "Who are you with?"

Meyer didn't answer her question, but he claimed she had called Child Protective Services on him, a charge she denied. "You child-trafficking piece of shit. Right here on a public road, I can stand here all fucking day, all fucking night, until you leave my kid alone. You piece of shit, Luciferian coward." Krause said she had never messed with his kid.

The 911 operator instructed Krause to remove the ammunition from her weapon before the sheriffs arrived. She still worried that his henchmen waited around the corner.

"They're on live video," he replied. "I got a deputy watching right now. Tell her [the 911 operator] to ask the deputy what I'm wearing. You're on live video, Rachel.

You can't hide anymore. I'm gonna stand right here, and I have not made one threat nor will I make a threat. I'm gonna expose you. I ain't here to hurt you. Why would I hurt you? Doesn't do me no good. I'll expose you; that's how we hurt you."

"Who dropped you off?"

"You don't worry about it. You don't worry about who's with me. You don't worry about where they are. Sheriff's Department, if they wanna worry about that, we'll talk with them when they get here, you fucking coward."

As Meyer hurled one accusation and insult after another, she thought of her daughter back inside. *Does she hear this? Is she scared?*

"She has sent the government after our families on sixteen occasions, and we have never ever come here," Meyer declared. "Now we come here. Now we come here every day if we have to."

Before the first squad car pulled up in front of her house, Krause told the 911 operator that she had removed the magazine from her gun. When the squad car inched up to the curb, Meyer was yelling at a female neighbor across the street.

Backup arrived, and a handful of deputies fanned out in the neighborhood. The officers spoke to Krause, interviewed her neighbors, and reviewed cellphone videos taken by a woman that lived nearby. They handcuffed Meyer and placed him in the back of a squad car. He continued yelling. "Pedophile," he screamed of Krause. "Meth head."

In Meyer's bag, the police officers found a large six-blade knife and a road flare. One officer carefully placed the objects in a brown paper sack and jotted them down as evidence. Another officer returned to the squad car. Meyer had calmed down and stopped yelling. The officer removed the handcuffs and re-cuffed them in front of Meyer rather than behind his back. They would take him to the police station and charge him with residential picketing and disorderly conduct, both misdemeanors, yet before the police wagon pulled off and headed to booking, an officer gave Meyer the phone he'd been using to record the standoff in front of Krause's home. Meyer made sure the video had posted on his Facebook.

———

I first met Krause in January 2019, when we sat down at a table in a crowded Denny's near downtown Tucson. She pointed to the pistol—the same one she'd grabbed when Meyer had stormed up to her home—fitted in a holster on her hip. "You don't mind that I have a gun, right?"

"Not at all," I told her. She'd taken to packing the gun after the incident a month earlier, fearing another unwanted confrontation could escalate to an attack on her.

Six months earlier, when Krause had first started tracking the VOP's activity, she simply wanted Meyer to stop parading around the desert and harassing people. Now, however, her goal had narrowed. "I want him arrested," she said. "Period."

She smiled while she spoke about the ordeal, recounting the previous six months over the din of the diner. A plate of eggs appeared on the table in front of her. Meyer was dangerous, she insisted. He could provoke a standoff or even a shootout, she said, alluding to the infamous 1992 Ruby Ridge shootout between a white supremacist holed up in a cabin and several federal agents. "I have no doubt that Lewis would not care if he died a martyr," she said, "because it would just feed a narrative. I don't think it would matter to him if he died because of it. As long as he gave his adoring public the so-called proof that it was all a conspiracy."

CHAPTER EIGHT
MAKING FRIENDS IN HIGH PLACES

Shortly after Tim Foley moved to Arivaca and set up shop in his double-wide right around the corner from the home where Brisenia and Raul Flores lost their lives, he found himself even more unwelcome in the town than he had been in Sasabe. La Gitana banned him, many townspeople shunned him, and antimilitia signs popped up on Arivaca Road, the main path bisecting town. "I've tried to talk to a couple of the people who oppose [us] and tried to have a nice dialogue with them," Foley claimed. "They just don't want it."

Having given up alcohol more than two decades ago, Foley didn't much mind that La Gitana had banned him. But in the months following Megan Davern's confrontation with Veterans on Patrol, word spread online like wildfire, sinking into the far-right crevices of social media. A steady stream of militias and vigilantes flowed through Arivaca in late 2018, and plenty of them showed up at the bar. Fresh from harassing the survivors of the Parkland mass shooting, the Utah Gun Exchange, a far-right online marketplace for weapons, had set up shop at La Siesta, a campground in Arivaca. And as Davern had done with Meyer and the VOP, she booted the Utah Gun Exchange, too, from the bar.

Davern and her colleagues at the bar fielded a storm of backlash and a string of hostile phone calls and Facebook messages, usually sent by militia supporters hiding behind the convenient cloak of anonymity. Utah Gun Exchange's cofounder Bryan Melchior, the man who had been rumbling up and down Arivaca's streets in an armored BearCat vehicle equipped with fake guns, attacked Arivacans while speaking to local media. "Arivaca is the most unwelcoming town I've ever been to in the United States of America," he told CBS5. "And I've been to almost every town of every state in this country."[1]

But with concern mounting, many in town were more worried by the threat that conspiracy theories posed to their safety than Arivaca's image as inhospitable. "I have never, ever felt threatened by a migrant, and I felt very threatened by militia," Davern told me. "These militias are based in racism and ignorance. And I have so much concern about people coming from other places, who don't know anything about the place . . . people who want to be martyrs because they don't lead very fulfilling lives."

The town held their another meeting in October, and more than seventy people turned out. By the time the meeting wrapped up, the attendees walked away with a plan: some people would track militia groups' online activity and hate speech, others would lobby local businesses to blackball the vigilantes, and an antimilitia sign would be placed prominently in town.

Around the same time Arivaca began organizing to push out the militias, Foley was busy cultivating important ties with a handful of local allies and right-wing politicians and anti-immigrant advocacy groups across the United States. In Phoenix and in Washington, DC, some state and federal lawmakers and officials lauded AZBR, welcoming Foley at rallies and press conferences.

While Foley's claim that he enjoyed the support of a "silent majority" of Arivacans seems implausible, he had secured valuable alliances. He struck up a friendship with Jim and Sue Chilton, local ranchers known for their ultra-conservative advocacy and ties to then president Donald Trump. The Chiltons, whose fifty-thousand-acre ranch hugged the border, regularly hosted Foley and other vigilantes. "They're ranchers, and cattle ranchers tend to be conservatives," Foley said of the Chiltons. "They know we can go into an area and create havoc for the cartel, which pushes them out of their area for a while."

On March 10, 2018, Foley joined a pro-Trump "Unity Rally" in Phoenix. There he shared the stage with former Maricopa County sheriff Joe Arpaio, whose long track record of civil rights violations had earned him pariah status among many but also fame among the far right.[2] Less than a year earlier, Trump pardoned Arpaio, who had served five terms in office, for a contempt-of-court conviction. Other participants included Kelli Ward, an Arizona state lawmaker backed by Trump and his former presidential advisor Stephen Bannon, and the Oath Keepers, one of the largest armed anti-government groups in the country.[3]

With the times changing in his favor, Foley traveled to Washington, DC, and participated in a press conference on Capitol Hill on September 7, 2018.[4] He joined the ranks of speakers including the White House counselor Kellyanne Conway, former National Security Advisory staff member Sebastian Gorka, and the Republican congressman Steve King. Also addressing the audience were so-called angel families: relatives of individuals killed by undocumented immigrants.

Foley, with his sun-faded neck tattoo peeking out from his collar, stood out among the suits and ties flanking him on both sides. He derided lawmakers over the flow of undocumented migrants into the country. "What's happening in that building is insanity," he said, motioning to the Capitol Building.

"I'll even make you an offer," he continued. "You give me that fifty-one billion [dollar budget], I guarantee you I shut that border within ninety days to everything and anything; you won't even get a bunny rabbit across that border." He lambasted depictions of Arizona Border Recon as a racist vigilante group that endangered migrants and gestured again toward the Capitol Building before closing: "Do your job."

———

The following day, Foley joined the second annual Mother of All Rallies, a gathering that counted among its headliners a slew of far-right figures, conspiracy theorists, and Trump associates. Among the riffraff was the day's most prominent speaker, Roger Stone, the nefarious political consultant who worked on several Republican campaigns—those of Richard Nixon, Ronald Reagan, and Bob Dole—and was often described as the mastermind behind Trump's 2016 presidential campaign.

When his turn to address the crowd came, Foley recycled a less polished version of the same speech he delivered a day earlier. "Nothing but shitbags" crossed the border into southern Arizona, he insisted. Migrant children introduced measles, mumps, and "everything that we wiped out in this country" into public schools, he added, echoing decades of xenophobic propaganda that painted foreigners as malignant diseases invading the once-healthy nation.

He concluded his speech by calling on the crowd to join him in a chant. "Build that wall! Build that wall! Build that wall!" The crowd, though small, joined in: "Build that wall! Build that wall! Build that wall!"

———

In the months that followed the town meetings, Arivaca locals opposing the militia painted more antimilitia signs and wrote letters to law enforcement, appealing for guidance and assistance in ridding their community of the militia threat. Around noon on December 2, 2018, a few cars bounced down the dirt road and pulled into the parking spots next to Arivaca's historic schoolhouse, a triangular tin roof sealing the top of the single-room rectangle made of adobe bricks painted a dull egg white.

Clouds like unruly gray thickets hung low and carpeted the sky. Arivaca's resident firebrand, Clara Godfrey, puffed a cigarette under a pavilion with a handful of townspeople before the meeting. Beyond them, slipshod shacks and disparate double-wides dotted a field adorned with trees, their winter branches sparsely leafed. When the stragglers arrived, everyone exchanged greetings, and Godfrey and the others finished their cigarettes and headed inside. Altogether, eighteen people trickled into the schoolhouse, taking seats at metal folding chairs arranged in a broad oval. Some reviewed notes they had prepared for the discussion. Megan Davern sat with a notepad on her lap.

As during the first town meeting, Godfrey stepped up first. She addressed the concerns she had heard in recent weeks.

"When that [antimilita] sign was put up, it bothered a lot of people," she said. She felt frustration, she added, because more people were outraged by the sign than by "a murder that took place in our community." She paused, surveying the room. "Well, that sign was stolen on Monday night."

Some townspeople worried that provoking the militias could prompt them to target Arivaca, she acknowledged, but hadn't they already targeted Arivaca? Turning in a slow circle to meet eyes with each of the attendees, she gestured energetically with her arms. "The shit's gonna hit the fan eventually. We have to know that. This is like a pimple; it's gonna bust at some point."

The attendees green-lighted a proposal to erect more antimilitia signs in Arivaca. Dan Kelly, a seventy-three-year-old retiree and army veteran, offered supplies—paint, wood, and tools—to put together more antimilitia signs. Anyone who wanted to join him when he designed his sign was welcome to come to his place, he said. Kelly had moved to Arivaca two years earlier, and he spoke out against the militias each time press came to town, often ravaging Foley as an army deserter coasting on stolen valor. ANOTHER VETERAN AGAINST THE VOP, his sign would declare from the metal gate hemming his property.

The crowd floated more ideas about what to do next. With Meyer and the VOP losing their online crowdfunding accounts and social media pages, they decided to keep up on the pressure online, and with the militia groups angered by La Gitana's no-entry policy, they agreed to lobby other businesses to adopt similar measures.

But not every local business had been willing to take a stand. Arivaca Mercantile, the local grocery store, had rebuked their appeals to decline Foley's business, as did the Artists' Co-op, the members of which politely declined to become entangled in what they viewed as divisive town politics. For her part, Godfrey wouldn't go to the businesses that allowed Foley and other militiamen. "The reason I don't go is because I don't want to confront these people in those places," she said. "It's not hate for the Merc or anything like that. They have to make their choice, too, and we need to respect that. But I can't go in there and be intimidated inside there because of the choices they've made. Now, the only control I have of is the corner [her property]. And Tim Foley will not come on the corner. That's that."

Dan Kelly urged people with "voices that would never get heard" to speak to a documentary filmmaker with whom he said he'd been in touch.

"Is she just wanting to get how we feel about them coming into our community?" a woman asked from the far corner of the classroom.

"Yeah," Kelly answered. "That's exactly what she wants. There's no angle."

Davern intervened with a raised hand. "I just wanted to say that there's always an angle."

"Whatever comes out of my mouth, I don't have a problem with anybody repeating it," Godfrey said.

Another woman shifted the focus of the conversation, directing a question to Terry Sayles. "Terry, have there been any repercussions for him emptying the water containers out there? I'm curious. Is there nothing anybody can do about it?"

"No, no, there was a suggestion of having the guys from Redneck Revolt [a left-wing militia] go out there and guard it, and [locals] said no, don't do that," Sayles replied. "If he empties it, he empties it." His answer revealed a serious problem. If law enforcement wouldn't take action against attacks on water tanks, what could be done? Suggestions like bringing in a left-wing militia to guard the water drops may not have gained much currency in Arivaca, but no one seemed to have a definitive answer of how to confront the problem.

The meeting dribbled to an end, and Godfrey summed up the day's sentiments: "This isn't left, this isn't right, this isn't boy, girl, nothing. This is right and wrong, and I want it to stay that way. Everybody has their own heart and why we're here doing what we're doing. But we're not doing it for any other reason than the truth, the truth about us as a village. We are not the cartel. We are not the monsters we're being portrayed to be."

She turned to the humanitarian activists who were present. "And the humanitarian group, I wanna say, I get a lotta schlop about you guys all the time, and this is my answer to it. I say, 'You know, there's never been a murder committed by the humanitarian group in our community.'"

"That's true," one of the activists replied. A few people laughed, and then everyone prepared to leave. The attendees put the chairs up and set out.

In the weeks that followed, three new signs popped up on Godfrey's lot. Like the original stolen sandwich board, each of the new, freshly painted white signs bore a circle and slash over the word MILITIA. A pair of cheeky words was written in cursive glitter paint on the bottom of one of the signs: THANK YOU!

A few days later, Godfrey found the sign battered and knocked over, tire marks smeared on it. She couldn't say whether the car-ramming was intentional, but she had her suspicions. She fixed it that same day.

I knew that some Arivaca residents thought it better to take a hands-off approach, in order to avoid provoking Foley or other militiamen. On a crisp morning in early January 2019, I drove to visit Rich Glinski, a former game warden who had moved to town after retiring a couple of years earlier. His home was perched on high ground and we could see the San Luis Mountains in the distance, rising like an immobile wave. Sitting in his living room, we spoke over coffee, and he explained the way he saw it. A couple of times a week, migrants would cross his property while heading north, but that didn't bother him. He understood that people needed help and that anyone would seek safety for their families. If he ever felt that danger threatened the lives of his children, who were now grown, would he not do the same thing? Wouldn't I? He thought Trump's border wall amounted to an awful idea, one that did nothing but further stoke hatred and division in an already deeply polarized country. But in recent years, he had developed a laissez-faire approach to conflict, believing that if one took a step back, tried to consider someone else's position, and refused to become angry, just about any problem could be solved. He'd converted to Buddhism and sought to cultivate a deeper capacity for empathy. He'd been especially touched by "This is Water," the popular commencement speech that the author David Foster Wallace delivered at Kenyon College in 2005. Although Wallace later tragically committed suicide, his life's work gained an impressive cult following, and "This is Water" became the sort of mantra-riddled essay cherished by many of his fans, including Glinski, those who dreamed of a world in which people acted only with good intentions, with a little bit more compassion, and with a lot more empathy.

Glinski thought the antimilitia signs and the efforts to drum up support for banning militiamen from public businesses amounted to bad ideas. "People do dumb things when there is desperation involved—we don't want the militia desperate," he told me, explaining that he felt like marginalizing the militiamen was akin to "kicking a hornet's nest."

"So, you're saying you fear—" I began.

"Not *fear*," he cut me off. "Never *fear*."

A few days later, Glinski picked me up in his white Toyota 4Runner. I hopped in, he handed me a small plastic cup of black coffee, and we headed out for the border. Although the frontier is only twelve miles from Arivaca, the ride was tedious, stretching more than an hour's time. We bounced down the road, my coffee spilling on my hand, passing the turnoff for Arivaca Lake, which sits off old Ruby Road and is maintained by the Arizona Game and Fish Department, for which Glinski once worked. We whizzed past barbwire fences lining property, some of them bearing NO TRESPASSING signs and others advertising solidarity with the No More Deaths activists being prosecuted at the time: HUMANITARIAN AID IS NEVER A CRIME, DROP THE CHARGES. I wondered if the signs were essentially emblematic of the roots beneath the current divide in Arivaca, if what it really came down to was that one group that believed in helping those in need, no matter where they came from, was facing off with another group that believed in protecting their own, shutting themselves off from the world around them, blacking out the suffering that existed—and persisted— outside their walls.

Glinski slowed down and stopped so that he could speak with the driver of a large pickup sauntering toward us. The driver rolled down his window, and Glinski greeted him: "You serve?"

The driver said he did, that he was a combat veteran, and Glinski thanked him. Then the driver, a man in his thirties wearing a weatherworn baseball cap, said he was scouting the area for hunting. He waved goodbye, and we started off again. I found myself contemplating how easy it would be to mistake commonplace hunters with militiamen, given that they often drive similar trucks, carry big guns, and wear camouflage. Even Glinski, wearing a camouflage cap and heavy-duty hiking gear, might pass as a militiaman. Only a day or two before our trip to the border I had seen a truckful of men, some middle aged and some younger than me, at the Mercantile, and weighed the probability that they were militia, at least until I saw a pile of dead animals in the pickup's bed.

The pavement ended and we continued slowly down a dirt road, well trodden and pocked with potholes. On the side of the road, a sign warned travelers: TRAVEL CAUTION— SMUGGLING AND ILLEGAL IMMIGRATION MAY BE ENCOUNTERED IN THIS AREA. We passed the entry to Ruby Mine, which was once a thriving mining community but now was advertised as one of southern Arizona's best ghost towns. Due to its remoteness, situated in a valley hemmed in by mountains, Ruby had attracted cattle rustlers and other outlaws. At its height, Ruby had been home to 1,200 people, a school, a post office, and a general store. In February 1920, a group of bandits—supposedly followers of the Mexican revolutionary Pancho Villa—escaped back into Mexico after they crossed the border, robbed the Ruby Mercantile, and killed the store's two owners.[5] Fourteen months later another raid took place, with Mexican bandits again bursting into the Ruby Mercantile and gunning down the new owner, Frank Pearson, and his wife, Myrtle, whose gold teeth they yanked out and made off with. In the summer of 1922, an Arizona deputy sheriff tracked down two of the men after a bartender in a Sonora, Mexico, cantina unsuccessfully attempted to sell him five gold teeth—Myrtle's—that an outlaw had given him. Manuel Martinez and Placido Silvas were put on trial and convicted of the murders, Martinez receiving the death sentence and Silvas a life sentence. In July of that year, Sheriff George White, accompanied by Deputy Sheriff L.A. Smith, was transporting Martinez and Silvas when he wrecked his police cruiser. Seizing the chaos of the moment, the prisoners freed themselves from their binds, murdered the police officers, and escaped into the desert. A crew of locals, the same ones who'd found White and Smith's bodies roadside, tracked them down in Mexico and brought them back north of the border. Martinez was hanged on August 10, 1923, and Silvas was sent to a prison in Florence, Arizona, to serve a life sentence. He escaped five years later and was never seen again, the story goes. The Ruby Mine continued to be profitable until 1941, when it was shuttered. Within a year the town was emptied of its residents.[6]

Glinski pulled off onto another dirt path, this one crawling up the face of a mountain, weaving nauseating loops around the risen earth. Our ascent was gradual, never topping five miles per hour, and we followed the trail spiraling around the mountain until we were near the top. From the crown of the mountain we could see snow-capped peaks in the distance, gulches collapsing into the earth, and yellow grass climbing up the sloping landscape. We drove on, Glinski explaining that he had conducted research in the area during the 1970s. He knew every species of tree, every species of bird's migratory patterns. He held the sort of knowledge I never knew I could envy—I know almost nothing about nature and cannot tell you the name of most trees, save for those of the palm and Christmas varieties.

We rolled up to an area where, deep down in a valley, a group of hippies had established a commune during the 1960s, on land that once housed Ruby's residents. The hippies had lived in teepees. During the biting winters, they tore down many of Ruby's homes, using the wood for fires and living on the land for several years. In 1971, the new owners of the land convinced the authorities to evict the hippies, some of whom simply migrated to Arivaca.

We finally reached the border, but it wasn't immediately apparent to me. I'd been to the border in San Diego, California, and in Texas's Rio Grande Valley, and I expected a sight like I'd seen in those places. In McAllen, Texas, and in San Diego, I had seen towering pipe fencing and barbwire. I recalled Border Patrol agents in Mission, Texas, whirring down the river on boats equipped with mounted guns. "Wait, this is it?" I asked Glinski, looking out at the cattle fence that divided the United States and Mexico. I could climb over it with a single hoist and hop, I thought.

"This is it," he said.

We moved on to an area called Casa Piedra, "the stone house." There was only a flood gate and some jerry-built cattle fencing. I walked around the remnants of a home that once stood there, a few pieces of stone foundation jutting out of the ground like teeth in a shattered smile. I moved to the fence, walked along it, and found a gate. I opened the gate and walked through, along a pathway bordered with scrap-wood walls. I hopped off an earthen step and landed in Mexico. I spotted a cluster of water jugs, canned food, and a few sacks of socks and clean clothes nestled on a stone ridge. Humanitarians had left them behind for people making the journey, and it struck me, after the lengthy trip that landed us here, how badly they would need them. I had no idea how long it would take to make this journey on foot, but I imagined it wasn't short.

BIENVENIDOS, someone had written on a water jug. *Welcome.* Another said, SIN FRONTERA, NO HAY EXILIO. *Without the border, there's no exile.*

Yet another, TEQUEREMOS, TE SENTIMOS, LA LIBERTAD ES TUYADESTINA. *We love you, we feel you, liberty is your destiny.*

"How are you going to build a wall way out here?" Glinski wondered aloud, following behind me. "It doesn't make any sense. You couldn't even transport the building material through those mountains."

It was true. The journey had taken us a solid hour to reach this spot, an area that Border Patrol, I imagined, rarely took the time to patrol. A small pipe floodgate stretched over a southward stream, and when the current picked up, it shot upward. Slapped together like a shanty house, with a crude combination of scrap wood, sheets of steel, and cattle fencing, the border here wasn't much. And yet it was too much, an arbitrarily drawn line that made little sense but divided human beings from their neighbors. The logic was as clear to me now as it had been a couple of years earlier, the first time I first stood on the Greek side of the Macedonian border in Idomeni, at a makeshift refugee camp that sprouted up when Macedonian border guards prevented people from continuing their journey to western

Europe. Without the fortified borders, without the need for smuggling and trafficking, those problems wouldn't exist. Without nefarious designations that labeled some people illegal and others permissible, there'd be no profits to be turned by shuttling people over the frontier. Later, in early 2020, tens of thousands of refugees gathered on the Greek-Turkish border. As they protested at the fence lining the frontier, I stood on a hilltop in Greece and watched border guards fire tear gas and flash bangs into Turkey, sending those protesting scattering. Meanwhile, Greek vigilantes gathered in militia-like groups, dusted off their guns, and patrolled the borderlands, chasing down refugees and, in one case, beating a reporter.

Back in Arivaca that night, I flipped open my laptop and started researching. After a couple of hours, I ended up deep down a rabbit hole on Arizona Border Recon's YouTube page. I watched one video after another of heavily armed men traipsing the desert. Then I landed on a video, captured on a trail cam, that caught my eye. In it, a group of fatigue-wearing men carrying heavy-duty firearms rode up on horseback to a cattle fence demarcating the border. They hopped down, tied up their horses, and climbed over the fence. Then I realized it was Casa Piedra, the same spot I'd been standing a few hours earlier. I wondered: *Does Tim Foley now have a video of Rich and me opening the gate?*

CHAPTER NINE
A SUSPICIOUS INDIVIDUAL IN THE DESERT

For much of the first half of 2019, Michael Lewis Arthur Meyer kept a low profile. In January, he briefly ceded control of Veterans on Patrol to another borderland vigilante and longtime VOP member, Rebecca "Becky" Ferland. She announced the creation of a splinter group, Arizona Desert Guardians. On a Facebook livestream later reposted on YouTube, Ferland said Meyer had "relinquished" VOP to her and two supposed military veterans. "We're going to be taking a full catalog of what was deeded over to us," she said. "We're not going to stop what we're doing just because Lewis is gone now. I invite people, the haters that have been after Lewis and VOP members for a while . . . we're inviting you guys to come down, meet with us, talk with us, because ultimately the kids come first, and we have got to start working together."

She urged new volunteers to join them in southern Arizona, emphasizing that although her newfangled group harbored no bad blood with Meyer, he would be going his own way. Explaining that she wanted to break away from the VOP's reputation and baggage, Ferland said, "We've decided that we're gonna change it to . . . Arizona Desert Guardians."

The separatist project was short-lived. By late spring, Meyer started popping up again around the desert, rearing his head from Tucson to Three Points. He continued operating under the VOP banner, and his hatred of Humane Borders and Joel Smith drove him to escalate his attacks on water stations. He graduated from vandalism to theft, outright tossing the water tanks in the back of his pickup and taking off with them. On Twitter, his posts grew increasingly paranoid and deranged, still tinged with the sort of aggression for which he had become well-known. The VOP account regularly accused Humane Borders's Smith of working for George Soros, Mexican drug cartels, and powerful Democratic political operatives. "Psst . . ." the group wrote on Twitter in July of that summer. "Someone tell @HumaneBordersAZ that their Supply Line for the Cartels and Sex Offenders are under attack."[1]

The types of conspiracy theories Meyer pushed were gaining more and more traction around the country. In July 2019, Yahoo! News published an FBI intelligence bulletin produced by the bureau's Phoenix field office, warning that conspiracy theorists increasingly presented a domestic terror threat. The bulletin predicted that conspiracy theories would inspire "both groups and individual extremists to carry out criminal or violent acts."[2] Worse still, the bulletin anticipated that conspiracy theorists would gain a larger audience heading into the 2020 presidential elections. After all, President Trump himself parroted one of the most prominent conspiracy theories of all: that migrants and refugees were "invading" the country via its southern border, a claim his campaign repeated more than two thousand times in Facebook advertisements between January and August of 2019.[3] The same rhetoric had recently reemerged in the manifestos of white nationalist killers around the world. In March of that year, a gunman stormed a pair of mosques in Christchurch, New Zealand, and murdered dozens of Muslim worshippers, whom he dubbed "invaders."

In August 2019, only five hours away from Tucson, Patrick Crusius opened fire in a Walmart in El Paso, Texas, and killed twenty-three people, citing in his manifesto a supposed "Hispanic invasion" of the state.[4] Roberto Jurado had been shopping with his eighty-eight-year-old mother when the gunfire rang out. Together, they took cover hiding in between toy machines near the store's entrance. Nearby, bodies were falling, and the gunshots were getting closer and closer, he later told the *El Paso Times*. The gunman, wielding an AK-47, got within ten feet of Jurado and his mother. "That day, I believe I stared death in the eyes," he said.[5]

"I think we all were [being targeted] because of the color of our skin," Jurado added. He was right. Crusius had traveled across most of the state of Texas, driving from the northern Dallas suburbs to the border town and picking a store he knew would be full of Latino shoppers.

In his rambling manifesto, which clocked in at more than two-thousand words, Crusius echoed the French writer and conspiracy theorist Renaud Camus, whose 2011 book *The Great Replacement* promoted the paranoid view that immigration to Europe was part of a global plot to undermine white Europeans and systematically replace them. His mantra had been adopted by the shooters in El Paso and Christchurch, and although he said he disapproved of the mass murders, he refused to disavow the notion he had put out into the world. "The great replacement has become a household word," he told a *New York Times* reporter. "I take responsibility for it. I believe in its relevance."[6]

But even if Camus had come out and disavowed his own ideas, it would have provided little solace to those who endured the bloodshed in El Paso. "I saw people crying: children, old people, all in shock," one witness said. "I saw a baby, maybe 6 to 8 months old, with blood all over their belly."[7]

———

Back in Arizona, rather than merely emptying the water tanks—knifing them and letting the water spill out onto the desert earth—Meyer had started hauling the blue barrels away in the bed of a pickup truck. He took to Facebook and Twitter to post videos showing the tanks in the pickup truck. The bragging came back to haunt him, however, when Pima County Sheriff's Department officers received a report of a "suspicious individual" in the Three Points area on August 6. The officers arrested him for alleged crimes related to the stealing and damaging of the water tanks, incidents that the department said had taken place three weeks earlier. Meyer was carted off to jail, booked, and charged with two felony counts of third-degree burglary and misdemeanor charges of criminal damage and theft. "We have had contact with Mr. Michael Lewis Arthur Meyer before," Deputy James Allerton told me by phone at the time. "I can't speak to how many reports [the sheriff's department received overall]. However, I know in the local area the [humanitarian] groups have complained about this sort of thing happening, and it's something our department has addressed. If a crime has occurred, our department is going to investigate that."

During the first half of 2019, militias and armed vigilante groups around the nation were wrapped up in high-profile court cases, some of them involving allegations that armed men planned to carry out murderous plots. On January 22, police arrested three men and a high school student after pulling them over and finding their vehicle loaded with twenty-three rifles and shotguns as well as three homemade bombs, which they allegedly intended to use in an attack on the Black Muslim community of Islamberg, New York.[8]

Two days after those arrests, two members of an Illinois-based militia pleaded guilty to five counts linked to their pipe-bomb attack on a Minnesota mosque, attempted bombing of a reproductive healthcare clinic, and armed robberies, among other charges. In August 2017, the men—twenty-nine-year-old Michael McWhorter and twenty-three-year-old Joe Morris—drove five hundred miles to Bloomington, Minnesota, and hurled a pipe bomb into the Dar al-Farooq mosque, causing an explosion but injuring no one.[9]

In April, a video clip of the United Constitutional Patriots, a New Mexico-based militia, detaining around two hundred migrants at gunpoint prompted widespread condemnation and led to the arrest of its leader, Larry Hopkins.

CHAPTER TEN
THIS IS AMERICA, AND I CAN LIVE WHEREVER I WANT

For years, authorities appeared to let Tim Foley operate without legal retribution—but only by a hair did he evade the sort of crackdown with which the government targeted other militia figures, and federal authorities appeared to be watching his group more and more closely. In January 2018, an enthusiastic Arizona Border Recon recruit, Joshua Pratchard, a thirty-eight-year-old veteran, hopped in his white Ford F-150, a 2018 four-door pickup, and drove nearly seven hours from his apartment in San Diego, California, to an AZBR camp in southern Arizona. Riled up about undocumented immigrants and looking for action, Pratchard showed up at the camp equipped with guns and a silencer. He submitted an application, saying he was drawn to the group because he "believed this was a way to give back to his country to help ensure that the border was not overrun by drugs, criminals and an invasion of illegal aliens," his attorneys would later say.[1]

His enthusiasm for detaining migrants belied a more harrowing truth: Pratchard had what prosecutors would later describe as "a long history of violence, and unresolved anger."[2] As a teenager, Pratchard had enlisted in the US Marine Corps. In 2001, at just nineteen years old, he was caught with fifteen ecstasy pills. The following year a military court convicted him on felony charges for using and selling ecstasy. Sentenced to three years in prison, he was granted a dishonorable discharge. In October 2007, after his release from the clink, he traveled to San Francisco for an Oktoberfest festival. Along with a pair of friends, Pratchard joined in a fight with another festival attendee. Pratchard and his friends beat the man, and when the victim hit the ground, the former Marine stomped on his face repeatedly. By the time law enforcement showed up and broke up the tussle, the victim was "lying in a pool of blood," having suffered a broken nose, a fractured jaw, and a concussion, court documents later showed.[3] Pratchard pleaded guilty to a single count of felony assault, earning a three-year probation sentence, and admitted that he had beat the man "within an inch of his life," the same court records noted.[4]

By the time spring 2014 rolled around, Pratchard and his wife, Melissa, had experienced "several incidents . . . where Joshua was aggressive with her," but he had never crossed the line into domestic violence, court documents said. On March 9, though, tensions were boiling over. That evening, they went to a church class, and Pratchard stormed out "because he felt that some of the things they were talking about in the class . . . he was doing," his wife later recounted. They went home, but Pratchard refused to speak to his wife. After a while she grabbed her notebook and took off on her bicycle for the beach. After writing in her journal for a while, Melissa returned home to find Pratchard still upset with her. They made up, and Pratchard went to another room to do homework. The truce was brief, and after a while, he returned to the room screaming at

Melissa. He hurled a pill bottle at her, and then grabbed her by the arms. She had five seconds to leave, Pratchard warned her, or he would hurt her. He picked her up and tossed her onto the bed.[5] Melissa threatened to call the police, and he said, "Go ahead." When the police eventually arrived, he was arrested for battery of a spouse, a charge that was later dropped because Melissa did not want to send him to jail.

Pratchard's felony convictions legally barred him from owning guns, but at some point, he had started building his own guns and giving them to friends and family members.

In January 2018, Pratchard showed up for his first and only border operation with AZBR. He had filled out an application and passed the armed group's background check, despite his prior felony convictions. During the operation, Pratchard wore a white helmet and PVS-14 night-vision goggles strapped to his head, and posed for a slew of photos with the other militiamen. He lasted only a few days before returning to San Diego, no longer allowed to participate in AZBR operations.[6]

An AZBR member who has since quit the group, Joey (a pseudonym), was alarmed by Pratchard's behavior and alleged comments about confronting rip crews. Joey called the FBI to tip them off about Pratchard and became a paid confidential human source—CHS in law enforcement parlance—for the FBI agent Ryan McGee.

McGee instructed Joey to maintain communication with Pratchard. For several months, Joey recorded phone calls, took screenshots of text messages, and recorded video and audio of in-person meetings with Pratchard. In April, Pratchard made plans to travel to Phoenix, where he planned to attend a baseball game, meet Joey and his wife, and sell Joey a homemade weapon that couldn't be traced. Pratchard couldn't make it, though, and Joey proposed another meetup in the near future. He told Pratchard that Global Intel, a company Joey claimed to work for, might be able to hire him—as part of a ploy to get Pratchard back out to Arizona.

Joey got close to Pratchard. When the pair patrolled the Arizona borderlands in April 2018, Joey intentionally kept their operations limited to areas they were unlikely to spot migrants in, as per McGee's instructions. At the time, Pratchard told Joey he looked forward to confronting rip crews. "Does this mean we get to engage rip crews?" he asked, according to transcripts later presented in court.[7]

"More likely than not," Joey responded. "Not looking forward to it."

"I am," Pratchard said. "I want to do it."

On one occasion, Joey traveled to San Diego and spent time at Pratchard's apartment, where the former Marine had been building homemade weapons and ammunition. During that meeting, Joey recorded Pratchard speaking to his dog. "Who's that?" he urged the dog, ostensibly demonstrating that he had trained the pet to attack on command. "Go get him. Go get him. Go get that Mexican."[8]

More damning still, Joey recorded Pratchard discussing in detail his illegal gunsmith business based out of his home. "Do you know how many Blackout rifles you could buy if you stop smoking?" Pratchard asked Joey.

"As many as you can make," Joey replied.

"Exactly."

In another conversation, Pratchard revealed that he made short-barreled rifles and other weapons, often using his wife's and toddler son's birthdays as serial numbers. He could also make subsonic ammunition designed to be fired at speeds below the sound barrier, which allows a gunman to fire without the loud *crack* noise that usually accompanies gunfire.

"Dude, that's some ammunition," Joey said. "It's hard to fucking find."

"Yeah," Pratchard answered. "That's why I make mine."

By the time Pratchard drove his Ford pickup to Casino Del Sol, a popular gambling resort in Tucson, at around 8:45 a.m. on June 1, 2018, he had already sold Joey two weapons, and ammunition. In the truck with him he was carrying a cache of firearms and ammunition. Yet as he swung into the casino's parking lot, police lights appeared in his rearview. Federal agents emerged and served him with an arrest warrant. Searching his truck, the agents retrieved a short-barrel rifle, a standard rifle, a pistol, and 290 rounds of ammunition. They also located a tactical vest equipped with bullet-resistant plates, a GPS device, a tourniquet, and a silencer.

More than four hundred miles away, warrant-waving federal agents dug through Pratchard's home, where they found the equipment he used to build guns as well as enough gunpowder to produce an estimated nine thousand rounds of ammunition.[9] When they opened a safe in the home, they found eight firearms: four registered to his wife, and four that were Pratchard's own handiwork.

Altogether, prosecutors hit Pratchard with thirteen counts of various charges: possession of firearms by a convicted felon; transferring firearms to an out-of-state resident; and possessing unregistered firearms. He pleaded guilty in February 2019, and in August, the court sentenced him to seventy-five months in a federal prison. Shackled and wearing an orange jumpsuit at the sentencing hearing, he addressed the judge: "This has been a difficult road for me and my family because of the choices I made. I made a really stupid decision . . . I got so wrapped up in the ability to build them, not necessarily in using them. It essentially became my idol."[10]

Throughout Pratchard's trial, the prosecutors and FBI agent Ryan McGee made only passing mention of Tim Foley and AZBR. When the news of Pratchard's conviction broke in August, AZBR claimed that the group had kicked him out for wanting to detain migrants and carrying a silencer. I still had questions, though. How had Pratchard passed AZBR's background check? And was there any evidence they had ejected Pratchard from the group? I tried to ask, but they never returned my calls.

———

One day in October 2019, Rachel Krause called me with a tip. Since Michael Lewis Arthur Meyer had been arrested, she had shifted much of her focus to Tim Foley and the Arizona Border Recon. A couple of evenings earlier, she had been digging around on AZBR's Facebook page when she spotted an interesting comment. Someone posting from the AZBR account had published a status update accusing a former member, Red (a pseudonym), of being the federal informant who had passed on information about Joshua Pratchard. Joey told me he had replied with a comment saying that Red wasn't speaking with the feds—it was him who'd phoned the FBI to warn them about Pratchard and later acted as a plant for the agency. Krause quickly messaged Joey, and after reaching out to Red, he replied to her request to chat.

She wanted to connect me with Red. "Can I pass on your contact?" she asked.

"Of course," I told her.

When Red finally phoned me, we ended up speaking for nearly four hours. I was initially skeptical, but I could tell from his literacy in the inner workings of AZBR that he had been an actual member of the group. But he couldn't answer all of my questions. "You need to talk to Joey," he told me.

In late September, I drove from Dallas to Tucson to set up a meeting with the Joey and Red. A few days later, on a Sunday, I picked up Rachel Krause near a McDonald's in Marana at 7:30 a.m., and we set off for an Iron Skillet diner attached to a truck stop in Casa Grande, a city situated on I-19 about halfway between Tucson and Phoenix.

In his fifties and residing a few hours away from the Phoenix area in a southwestern Arizona community, Joey told me he first reached out to AZBR after seeing *Cartel Land*, a film that inspired the "majority of people who signed up," he recalled. "That's what got me hooked."

Before watching *Cartel Land*, Joey had little idea about cartel activity on the US-Mexico border. Feeling that Border Patrol lacked manpower, he viewed Foley and his bandits as a group of dedicated patriots filling in the gaps. *Wow*, he thought. *He's trying to help out the Border Patrol by going places where they don't have manpower and stop drugs from coming across the border. I'm down for that. Drugs are bad, right? The cartel's bad.*

After passing AZBR's background check, Joey officially became part of the group. A few months after his first border operation in November 2016, Joey helped Foley relocate from Sasabe to Arivaca. Joey had never heard of the 2009 murders in Arivaca, and Foley never told him, he said. One day Foley phoned Joey and warned him of the trouble brewing in town.

"They know we're in Arivaca now," he said, according to Joey, "and they don't like it."

Now out of the group and harboring a grudge, Joey cast doubt on Foley's motivation for choosing Arivaca: "The Shawna Forde thing, he knew. He knew all about [the murders]. He could have moved anywhere when he got kicked out of Sasabe, but he chose Arivaca . . . because he knew he could keep his name out there. Even if it was bad, his name would still be there . . . That's how he gets paid—notoriety."

Although he had served in the military, Joey found himself grappling with a "steep learning curve." Because the armed group provided meager training, much of the preparation and training was left for Joey to figure out for himself. Land navigation and tracking were skills he took it upon himself to learn. Worried about the flow of drugs across the border and impressed with the group's ability to attract military veterans and law enforcement—around 8 percent of recruits, Joey estimates—he was willing to put in the extra time. He eventually climbed the ranks of AZBR and became Foley's de facto second in command.

Over time, however, red flags appeared. With one unsavory person after another showing up at AZBR operations, Joey began to grow suspicious of the group's background-check procedure. On the fateful day that Joshua Pratchard arrived, he did a quick Google search on his iPhone and found Pratchard's felony convictions from years earlier. Worse still, Joey felt like the operations were primarily geared toward media as "a big dog and pony show" charging each outlet $200 a day. During operations, he was confused by some participants who covered their license plates. He asked why they did so, and he soon learned that they feared informants in the group. As the following months wore on, even more cracks formed in Joey's resolve. Joey kept attending operations every few months, but he gradually realized AZBR's impact paled in comparison to its reputation as a band of border enforcers. He rarely saw scouts and drug runners in the desert, and he guessed that they avoided the areas AZBR frequented.

During one operation in February 2017, however, Joey and a few others happened upon three scouts, or cartel lookouts. No one had informed Joey that they weren't legally allowed to detain people, and when the trio tore off in the desert, Joey and the others gave chase. It crossed his mind that the men may have been armed, but he pursued them anyway. He recalled his thoughts to me: "We're going to jump these dudes, throw them on the ground, and wait for Border Patrol." The men were too quick for the militia and they eventually escaped. "These guys could run forever," he said. He was heaving from the sprint and he gave up. The men had left behind a bag full of weed, food, and handheld radios. "I was like, man, I want some more of this," he recalled. "I want to catch these guys. Turns out [running into them] was sheer luck—it wasn't any skill on [Foley's] part."

Later on, he reflected on the chase, and it all began to set in. He could have been shot. He could have hurt someone and have wound up facing charges. "There's no training involved . . . You don't know what these guys are going to do, which is dangerous," he told me. "I'm surprised somebody hasn't gotten killed already doing this shit. That's what bothers me."

More often than not, Foley and others raided the humanitarian aid supplies left behind, stealing canned food, bags of Cheez-Its, and bundles of socks left behind by aid groups. When Tim Foley and his followers crossed the border carrying weapons, Joey grew paranoid. Could they spark an international incident? One of the final straws came when Joey learned that AZBR's Randon Berg had participated in rip crews and was suspected of ratting out others to federal agents to avoid catching a much heftier sentence, one that would have surely seen him relegated to a prison cell.

One day in summer 2018, Joey joined an operation in southern Arizona, lugging his heavy bag of equipment in the desert. The sun bore down. He had been in AZBR for nearly two years, and there in the desert, he had what he remembers as a "freaking heatstroke epiphany." Foley spent most of the time during operations palling around with media and driving, and he wouldn't have been the one on the chopping block. If something went wrong and the law got involved, Joey realized, it would be him—not Foley—facing charges. "You can't detain these guys," he said of the migrants they targeted. "You can't do anything to them . . . Who would get in trouble? *I* would be in trouble. *I* would be in jail."

When he returned home after the operation, Joey made up his mind: he was done with AZBR. He wrote a lengthy resignation letter and emailed it to Foley. "Tim tells everybody, 'We're not a militia, we're an NGO, we're an intelligence gathering operation,'" said Joey. "But he's a militia—he's no different than the Three Percenters or any other crazy militia running around out here . . . I don't think there's a militia down here that's not fucked up. They've all got some anti-government bent. They're all trying to raise money. They're all fighting over territory. I mean, this is stupid."

———

Meanwhile, the conflict in Arivaca shed much of its momentum over time. Foley refused to leave town, and most in the community quit calling for his departure. His presence, it seemed, became a fact of life. The opposing sides in town gradually reached an uneasy standoff. Michael Lewis Arthur Meyer was tangled up in legal drama elsewhere, locked up in a Pima County jail, and Tim Foley was playing the long game, avoiding public confrontations, and spending most of his time split between his double-wide and the desert.

When I spoke to Foley by phone in January 2019, he insisted that he had no plans to leave Arivaca. "They [the residents] can cry all they want, but last time I looked, this is America and I can live wherever I want," he said. "They're crying so much about this because they're afraid now that there's somebody in their backyard watching . . . and they're afraid of being caught."

Foley paused, and then added, "I was here through Obama and I'm here through Trump. I'm not going anywhere until I feel the place is secure."

By all indicators, Foley didn't appear to be leaving anytime soon. According to Internal Revenue Service documents, he obtained 501(c)(3) nonprofit status for his organization—registering it as AZBR Vets Inc.—in late

2018. The move fit into Foley's larger plan of creating a getaway space for military veterans—and it added further institutional legitimacy to AZBR's operations. Eight years after Foley struggled to launch his group and claimed to have laced the desert with improvised explosive devices (IEDs), he was listed as the chairman of the board of directors for AZBR Vets Inc.

In late 2019, however, I woke up one morning to a curious text message from Megan Davern. "Hey," it read. "Looks like Jan Fields is selling her property, and Tim is getting booted off." I clicked on the link she'd sent with her note. It led me to Zillow, an online real estate website. Advertised at $75,000, the ten-acre property listing included eighteen photos. The photos showed the winding dirt paths crisscrossing the property, often with Tim Foley's pickup and double-wide in the background, and the distant blue-tinted mountains puncturing the clouds. "Beautiful opportunity for the person wanting horse property, views of mountains, and grass land," the listing read. "Currently there is a tenant in mobile . . . The mobile [home] and any personal property are not included in this sale." Some locals in Arivaca thought it meant Foley was on his way out, but in the end, he had no plans to leave town.

CHAPTER ELEVEN
I USED TO BE A SHITBAG

The world, including Arivaca, was in lockdown as COVID-19 continued to spread. With the sun beating down at just over eighty-five degrees on the beaming blue day of June 8, 2020, Veterans on Patrol returned to Arivaca with a pick-up-truck bed full of garbage bags bursting at the seams. On its Facebook page, the group posted a video along with a comment directed at the "Liberal #Shitbags" in the border town, whom the group predictably accused of supplying "the Illegals" in the area. All of the trash, the post suggested, would be dumped in "Cartel-friendly" Arivaca.

The video begins with someone off-screen reading from a note printed up in Spanish. "This area is being monitored by Veterans on Patrol," says Meyer: "Smuggling and illegal trafficking of women, children, and drugs is no longer permitted. This route is closed."

The camera phone zooms in on the humanitarian aid office across the street from La Gitana. "That's Humane Borders in Arivaca," the unidentified voice says, inaccurately. The camera zooms back to the bed of the pickup truck. Black plastic sacks are piled up in the bed, held down by rope ties. "This is all the illegal drug-trafficking, human-trafficking trash we've been picking up out there in Three Points. It all originates right here, and it's because of that humanitarian aid office."

"I'm going to show you guys something else," the cameraman says, the camera bouncing back toward the entry of the bar. He directs the camera down toward the door sign barring militias and other groups just as the door flings open.

"Can I help you with something?" says an employee who appears in the doorway.

"Yeah, I'm looking at your sign."

"Cool. Take it all in."

"Why aren't these people allowed?"

The employee sighs loudly and lets the door fall shut. "Really?" the cameraman says, laughing. "You fucking bleeding-heart liberals." Right before the camera clicks off, the reflection in the door shows who had been speaking behind it all along. It was Paul Flores, a self-described journalist who increasingly had been participating in VOP activities for months. When Flores later posted the video on YouTube, he dubbed Arivaca the "most unpatriotic town in America."

———

After Michael Arthur Lewis Meyer's August 2019 arrest in Three Points, he sat in county jail for months. Although the charges stemming from the Three Points incident had been dropped, Meyer was not released until April 2020: he was held for violating conditions related to prior charges. After he was cut loose, Meyer set out on a warpath like never before. Arizona, the country, and much of the world were struggling to deal with the coronavirus pandemic fanning out the globe over.

He quickly linked up with Paul Flores, who was running

the somewhat popular Darkskywatchers Global Skywatch Network page on Facebook. With nearly two thousand likes, Flores had carved out a niche disseminating hyperbolic and sensational reports related to immigration, often pushing VOP's conspiracy theories about the supposedly ominous forces working behind the scenes. Working together, Flores and Meyer covered ground all over Pima County, from Three Points to Arivaca. On both of their Facebook pages, Flores and Meyer posted a slew of videos pushing some of the most wild-eyed anti-immigrant conspiracy theories to date. From the photos, statuses, and videos, it appeared that every piece of trash they chanced upon in the desert was indisputable evidence of the cartel's reach deep into the territory of the United States.

More alarming still, VOP ratcheted up the stakes. Rather than spreading misinformation about humanitarian water stations, vandalizing them, or stealing them, the group began setting up fake water stations as "bait" for migrants trawling across the desert. Flores often carried a weapon, and VOP's transformation from a supposed veterans' organization to a full-on militia seemed in full swing. On a near-daily basis, VOP social media posts urged Pima County residents to report undocumented people to Immigrations and Customs Enforcement. And while Lewis didn't shy away from accusing almost every public official in Pima County of colluding with drug cartels, he held an especially dogmatic grudge against Arivaca.

On June 10, a post on the VOP Facebook page claimed that "ARIVACA HELPS ILLEGAL SEX OFFENDERS," sharing a photo of an undocumented immigrant convicted on charges of sexual abuse of a minor. Accompanying the photo was a link to a post on the Border Patrol's website.

The write-up confirmed that Border Patrol agents had captured the man near Arivaca, but curiously omitted any reference to the people of Arivaca helping him.[1] That same day, Lewis took to Facebook Live and recycled old claims about supposed rape trees in the desert and Pima County providing cover for the drug cartels. "If you come down here and ask anybody about which county is helping the cartel, they'll tell you it's Pima County," he said.

"Those water stations don't save lives," he continued, "because where those water stations are, water is available immediately in the area. You don't need to put one behind an elementary school. I mean, there's businesses. There's a fire station. There's two main highways right here. I mean, hell, you can just walk to the corner and flag [someone] down to get water. No, the water stations are used to conceal the coyotes and the traffickers that are running all the cargo up both sides of the border. Two-way routes. And they want to protect all the routes that are going back, taking the money and the weapons and sneaking that shit back into [Mexico]. You know, they gotta protect these certain routes. Now, these Humane Borders illegal trafficking routes—anyone can go and look at where they staged their flags and you will see. Zoom down on Google Earth. You'll find very few flags in isolated areas where there is not water available. I mean, we haven't found one yet, to be honest with you."

Shining particularly bright in Lewis's rant was a curious admission. "The people using these cartel water stations are shitbags," he said. "Now, I say that as a prior shitbag. Now, if I want to call them a shitbag—you haven't been a shitbag, then you don't know what you're talking about.

I USED TO BE A SHITBAG

Don't call 'em something you don't know. I know what a shitbag is. I used to be a shitbag. That's why we are really good at tracking these fuckers down."

———

By midsummer Meyer's descent into the shadowy world of alt-right and anti-Semitic conspiracy theories was in full swing. With each day that passed, VOP's social media posts grew more aggressive. In late May and early June, millions had risen and spilled into the streets to protest the police killing of George Floyd, an African American man, in Minneapolis, Minnesota. In cities and towns stretching from New York to Los Angeles, tens of thousands rallied in the streets, and police suited up in military-style gear and tried to quell the demonstrations. In some cases, riots erupted and stores were looted. Police officers all over the country deployed an iron fist, spraying protesters and reporters with tear gas and firing rubber bullets at them, among other so-called less-than-lethal crowd control tactics, and arresting people in troves.[2]

In his typical fashion, Meyer sought to capitalize on the tensions. With protests spearheaded by the Black Lives Matter movement, VOP began to post the hashtag "#ChildLivesMatter" on social media, even suggesting in one post that people should instead riot over the child sex trafficking he claimed to expose: "Did someone ask where all the Riots for the Children are?" he wrote on the VOP Twitter on June 14, 2020. Although the post added that VOP wouldn't "be Rioting," the group vowed to expose "the Crimes of Soros Puppets," tagging a list of Pima County officials. Among those included in the post were Tucson mayor Regina Romero; County Attorney Barbara LaWall; County Sheriff Mark Napier; Tucson police chief Chris Magnus; and County Administrator Chuck Huckelberry, whom Meyer described as the "highest paid Cartel supporter on the Border."

Along with the Soros delirium, Meyer posted a flurry of tweets and Facebook statuses that used the hashtag "#redpill," an alt-right nod to the film *The Matrix*, in which the protagonist must decide whether to take a blue pill—which would allow him to live life as normal—or a red pill—which would unveil the supposed truth of the world. On June 15, he again stepped it up a notch: he posted a video of people he alleged were federal agents—whose faces were out of frame—informing him that someone planned to kill him. A tirade on the VOP page began, "At this point, anything Lewis Arthur does short of Murder would be justified."

In a subsequent post on his personal Facebook page, he ticked off the names of eight individuals whose neighborhoods would "be seeing our Patriots soon." On top of the usual Pima County officials, he included the right-wing veteran Craig Sawyer, with whom he had once drummed up the Cemex conspiracy theory, and Rachel Krause.

Later that same morning, Krause contacted me via text message: "When I end up in a ditch somewhere, please remember—I did NOT suicide myself." At the end, she added a smiley-face emoji.

The title of a video dated July 3, 2020, suggested that Veterans on Patrol had escalated their anti-migrant vigilantism once again: "Previously Deported Criminal in Route [*sic*] to Robles Elementary School Intercepted by VOP."[3]Behind the phone, Meyer keeps the camera trained on a man who is sitting on the desert ground shoeless and exhausted, brush and desert trees shielding him from the summer sun. The man is speaking Spanish, attempting to communicate with Meyer, but the VOP leader repeatedly accuses him of pretending that he doesn't know English. "One minute we understand English, the next minute we don't speak [it]," the vigilante says.

"I don't have anything," the man says in Spanish. "I'm tired."

"So far I've got that you're from Mexico," Meyer says. "You came here. They sent you back. You're back here right now."

Whether the man told Meyer where he came from before he started filming isn't clear. Meyer attempts to sprinkle Spanish into the conversation, but what comes out is mostly garbled and meaningless.

"I'm not carrying anything," the man says back. "I'm very tired."

He is a small man, dressed in a weatherworn polo and dirty jeans, and he pleads for more water. Meyer orders him to roll up his sleeves and show his tattoos. Explaining that Border Patrol is on the way, Meyer makes a startling admission while speaking to the man. "That was a long run," he says. "You're short and fast, and I didn't have an easy time getting you, so I'm not going to run again either."

Around four and a half minutes into the video, another man appears in the frame and gives the migrant a couple more bottles of water. Meyer's pal informs him that Border Patrol has arrived, and Meyer boasts to his audience. "Heading straight to the elementary school," he says. "Intercepted by VOP. Great job, guys. Not today. Stop child trafficking. Secure the border . . . Border Patrol is here. We're cutting the video."

In another video that summer, Meyer shows off a dog he had used to hunt down people in the desert.[4] He says the dog's name was Hans Solo (apparently mistaking this for the *Star Wars* protagonist Han Solo's name). The text accompanying the video says the canine had been trained to help locate houseless veterans—but how a dog, even the best trained among them, could differentiate between veteran and a nonveteran, a houseless person or a camper, he never explains. In any case, Hans Solo has a new mission. "Now he tracks #cartelshitbags," Meyer writes, "and he's good at it."

Meyer's usual claim was that his goal was to prevent drug smuggling and child sex trafficking, but the video only shows the dog tracking down backpacks with blankets, canned food, and clothes—items that give no hint of their owner: drug smuggler, human trafficker, asylum seeker, American camper. In one clip, Meyer opens up a pack and celebrates the big find: "a whole food stash . . . a lot of good eatin'." At another point in the video, the camera zooms in on the face of a man sitting on the side of the road, a saguaro standing tall behind him. "Solo will find you," the text warns, "and you will get caught . . . Not today, shitbag."

Never mind that he had no military or law enforcement experience. Meyer used the footage as a promotional tool, a recruiting video that encouraged others to travel to the border and join his quest to combat child sex traffickers and cartel members. "Join Screwy Louie and Hans Solo," the video concludes. The VOP leader continued to tell on himself, but no one prevented him from detaining and harassing people in the desert.

A separate video, with a similar soundtrack of grating electronic music, depicts Meyer, Paul Flores, and others walking around in a trash-flecked mine somewhere in southern Arizona.[5] "Cartel Dope Mine Shut Down," the title claims, but neither drugs nor evidence of the mine being used by cartels appears. Instead, the vigilantes pick up old sun-battered water jugs and plastic bags and stuff them all into burlap sacks. "This place is closed," Meyer says. "A long three days," he adds, apparently explaining how long it took them to clean up the mine. At the end, a caption calls on supporters to volunteer with the vigilante outfit, urging others to "mobilize to Pima County" and providing an email address, underneath which is a pair of hashtags: #OpSia and #WWG1WGA, a QAnon-inspired hashtag that meant "where we go one, we go all." The line was ripped from the 1996 film *White Squall*.[6]

In July 2020, Twitter cracked down on QAnon-linked accounts, and the VOP page disappeared shortly after.[7] The tech giant deleted more than 150,000 such accounts, but the conspiracy theory was making headway offline. In Colorado that month, a QAnon promoter clenched the Republican congressional primary, securing her candidacy for the elections scheduled to take place four months later. At the time, the watchdog Media Matters for America estimated that there were at least twenty-three candidates who embraced the conspiracy theory.[8] Facebook had already scrapped some QAnon-inspired accounts, but it wouldn't be until October of that year that the social media outlet entirely banned the conspiracy theory among its users. "Starting today, we will remove Facebook Pages, Groups and Instagram accounts representing QAnon," the company said in a press release. "We're starting to enforce this updated policy today and are removing content accordingly, but this work will take time and will continue in the coming days and weeks."

The release continued, "Our Dangerous Organizations Operations team will continue to enforce this policy and proactively detect content for removal instead of relying on user reports."[9]

Online and off, the conspiracy theory was entrenching itself into American society as time went on. *The Guardian* published a list of violent incidents linked to QAnon that stretched back to June 2018.[10] But the number of incidents surged in 2020: of the twelve examples, seven had taken place between March 2020 and October 2020. The first incident involved a Kentucky woman named Neely Blanchard kidnapping her twin daughters—whose custody she didn't have—from their grandmother's house. The next month, a man hopped up on QAnon-adjacent conspiracy theories about the coronavirus attempted to derail a freight train in Los Angeles. In August, a Texas woman named Cecilia Fulbright crashed her car into two other vehicles while chasing someone she believed to be a child sex trafficker in Waco. Her relatives later told the website Right Wing Watch she believed Trump was "literally taking down the cabal and the pedophile ring," *The Guardian* report noted.

Back in Arizona, Meyer continued promoting the con-spiracy theory. His videos were almost always accompa-nied by the QAnon hashtag, and he wanted more people to join him on his patrols.

CHAPTER TWELVE
ELECTIONS, RIOTS, THE BORDER, AND THE FUTURE

It was early November 2020, and I had returned to Arizona to follow the presidential elections. Rumor had it that militia groups were gearing up to intimidate anti-Trump voters at the polling stations, and that tensions had hit a fever pitch. Leading up to the vote, I drove from Tucson to Arivaca and from Arivaca to Phoenix, speaking to voters about their hopes. For the first time since Bill Clinton won the state in 1996, there appeared a real possibility that a Democrat could win Arizona's eleven electoral votes. Clinton had bested the Republican candidate Bob Dole by only 2.2 percentage points, and Trump still commanded broad support in Arizona.

In Phoenix, I drove to the Epworth United Methodist Church, situated in a neighborhood in the northern part of the state capital. On the curb at the edge of the parking lot, cars passed signs that read FUCK TRUMP in Spanish and SUPPORT MIGRANT FAMILIES in English. A steady stream of voters parked their cars and sauntered toward the church. Volunteers directed their way to go to cast their ballots, and a nonprofit group handed out meals to anyone who came by—long lines had been expected, but the church had only a couple dozen voters at a time. A group of houseless men lingered behind a building next door, sometimes yelling. Out from the voting station came two young men, both white and both wearing Trump T-shirts. Justin, who was nineteen, had cast his vote for the first time ever. He ticked off a laundry list of reasons he backed the president: everything from the economy to supporting law enforcement. "The most important thing for me is obviously the economy—we need a strong economy," he told me. "And then law and order is a big thing for me."

His friend was a twenty-six-year-old college student, a business major named Robert. Robert had voted for Trump four years earlier, and he repeated that choice that day. In addition to lower taxes, he wanted the president, if reelected, to clamp down on Black Lives Matter. "The civil unrest and everything—I feel like there needs to be something done," he said. On top of that, Robert believed Trump would soon put an end to the monthslong lockdown put in place to protect against the spread of the COVID-19 coronavirus. "Trump is going to be the one to stop the lockdown," he added. "I think it's time everybody goes back to work."

Across town, at Glendale Community College, the voting line was growing longer throughout the afternoon. Environmental activists handed out flyers and begged voters to sign their petitions. A progressive Jewish group sat at a table and offered advice to anyone who would stop long enough to listen. And in the parking lot, a group of Trump supporters, mostly older people, set up a pair of tables and urged passersby to reelect the incumbent Republican. One table advertised a new splinter party— pro-Trump but anti-Republican establishment, they insisted—while the other passed out placards that read LATINOS FOR TRUMP. They complained about political correctness and Nancy Pelosi. They bickered about the coronavirus lockdown and insisted COVID-19 wasn't real. And every now and then, the conversation veered to QAnon, the supposed whistleblower who had inspired a nationwide conspiracy theory: the mass delusion that claimed Trump was engaged in a clandestine battle with child sex traffickers who occupied the upper echelons of the Democratic Party.

Francine Romesburg, a longtime Tea Party activist, lingered around the Trump tables throughout the day. She was convinced that a steal was already underway, that the Democrats had rigged the election and that the media was playing its part dutifully by projecting a Biden win. "The polls are never correct," she told me. "They weren't even close last time—and they're not close again." Along with her husband, Romesburg had launched a fledgling right-wing party that sought to siphon hard-line Christian conservatives from the Republican Party, a goal borne from their shared belief that the party had betrayed Trump. She dismissed most GOP leaders as RINOs, "Republicans in name only," and hoped her party—known as the Arizona Patriot Party—would eventually gather enough support to run its own candidates. "We are prepared to support Republicans, but only if they're constitutional," she said, explaining that anyone who cared about "truth, honesty, our freedom, our liberties, our religion," would vote for Trump.

Yard signs on the college's lawn urged voters to wear masks and maintain a six-foot distance between one another, guidelines designed to prevent unnecessary spread of the coronavirus. But Romesburg and her group ignored them. She knew the entire pandemic was a global plot to undermine individual freedoms, she said.

A young man in a MAKE AMERICA GREAT AGAIN hat walked out of the voting station, stopping to chat with those gathered in the parking lot. His name was Blake Spanko, and he was twenty-two. Walking to his car, he told me Trump would put an end to abortion, the most important issue in the nation for a "traditional Christian" like himself.

None of their reasons for backing Trump were surprising. Republicans around the country had repeated them for four years. Many issues—abortion, supporting law enforcement, lower taxes—had been staples of the Republican Party's platform for decades, long before Trump took the reins and morphed the GOP into a party with outward sympathies for white nationalists and conspiracy theorists.

What stood out as novel was the extent to which Trump supporters bought into it all, how willing they remained to exact violence in order to keep their man in office. That night, vigilantes gathered outside the electoral commission building in Maricopa County, where they insisted that Trump ballots weren't being counted. Around two hundred armed vigilantes and militia types had assembled outside the electoral building, waving AR-15s and claiming that the Democrats had stolen the election from Trump and the Republican Party. The AZ Patriots, a hard-line pro-Trump group, walked right into the building at one point.

Meanwhile, conspiracy theories, some pushed by the president himself, crawled out from the seedy crevices of the Internet and were fanned out on social media. Even before Election Day, Trump's far-right base had targeted people in the streets. Two days before the vote, four Trump supporters mauled and beat a man in Tucson, an incident caught on tape.[1] On Election Day, sixty-three-year-old Robert Norwood was spray-painting anti-Trump graffiti on his own property when he was confronted by a man who thought he was committing an act of vandalism—he died in the brawl that ensued.[2]

On November 5, a crowd reassembled outside the electoral commission building. Alex Jones, the Texas-based conspiracy theorist and founder of InfoWars, had made the journey from Austin. With his signature megaphone, he delivered a tirade that riled up his fellow Trump supporters. "Resistance is victory. You are victory!" he told the crowd. Cheers flashed through the flag-waving swell of people. "I salute you!"[3] Later, they chanted "1776," as if Trump himself had created the Republic.

The protesters continued coming out each night. On the fourth consecutive day, I drove back to Phoenix and parked down the street. MAKE AMERICA GREAT AGAIN hats bobbed over the sea of demonstrators, the late afternoon wind danced through American flags and Trump flags, and all around stood protesters decked out in tactical gear. Almost no one wore a mask. Some held AR-15s close to their chests. The police had erected a chain-link fence as a barricade between the protest and the press—a group of demonstrators had taunted journalists so intensely that authorities felt violence was imminent. "Four more years," the demonstrators sang. "Back the blue," they later chanted.

Protesters took turns giving speeches to the crowd, which continued to grow as the day drained of sunlight. Several railed about stolen votes, falsely claiming that the vote counters intentionally ignored ballots that had been filled out with Sharpie markers. The conspiracy theory had spread quickly online and spilled out into the real world outside the electoral commission building. It became known as SharpieGate, and Trump supporters insisted that the plot was integral to the Democratic Party's massive plot against the sitting president.[4] STOP THE STEAL, read signs outside the building with Sharpies taped to them.

It wasn't long before the demonstrators took aim at the press again. "We forgive you for being traitors to our country," one man shouted across the chain-link fence. He was kneeling, an assault rifle across his lap. The television crews stood around, some crew members smoking cigarettes, none responding to the crowd.

Meanwhile, the event organizer Adel Belgaied took control of the demonstration, manning the megaphone and being broadcast through speakers that blasted his voice throughout the crowd. In the past, Belgaied, who was from Scottsdale, had led rallies against child sex trafficking in the Phoenix area, in the spirit of QAnon. He riled the crowd against the journalists on the other side of the fence. "Putting up a fence to peaceful protesters in America . . . is that what our future looks like?" he said. "I live in Scottsdale, and when the [Black Lives Matter] protests came down there, and they rioted and looted, I didn't see any fences stopping anybody. But I see people that are stopped right now, that are fighting for their democracy and the righteousness of their country. I see people fighting for this country to be free."

Belgaied spoke at length, insisting that none of his fellow protesters had committed any violence. "I wonder why we're being censored. I wonder why the media is over there worried about the drama when they're not standing there looking at the future," he said. "Do they know? Maybe they know the future. All I know is I'm not a conspiracy theorist. I'm just a person that when you put [a] freedom-of-speech zone in front of my face, I start to wonder what country

I'm living in. The freedom-of-speech zone is the United States of America. It should disgust you inside to even think to yourself that a freedom-of-speech zone has to go up. It should disgust you inside when a people of faith and love and prayer, day after day, stand here behind a fence pleading for a legal count. It should disgust you inside that you're dividing America. This is not God's work."

Droning on for a long time, Belgaied eventually kneeled and led the audience in prayer. But the prayer was an unusual one, rife with conspiracy theories and patriotic clichés. Blue-and-black American flags—intended as a show of support for police—flickered around him. "Lord, we're simply here to fight for this country. We're here to appreciate this country. We're here to make sure that an honest and fair election is all that happens," he said. "Lord, a lot [of us] are confused why dead people's ballots are received, why it takes six hundred thousand votes to be counted in four days and they're still not finished. Lord, just a lot of things just aren't making sense, and all we want is transparency, and we ask that you give that to us."

He went on to claim that Trump was "fighting for us right now," meaning "the people that are standing here, the children that are being sex trafficked, the poor boy and girl that's being raped at this current moment somewhere here in the United States."

Belgaied continued his prayer, begging for blessings. "And God, as peaceful protesters—not protesters; we're sitting here asking for one simple thing—we ask you that the people here take down this wall that shows pure communism, and this freedom-of-speech zone."

When he finally reached the end, he concluded, "In God's name we pray. Amen."

Gathered around Belgaied, the crowd echoed him. "Amen," they shouted.

———

The lockdown had further radicalized militia groups around the country, including those far from the borderlands, feeding their fever dreams of an all-authoritarian state hell-bent on exploiting the pandemic to strip Americans of their constitutional rights. In October 2020, the FBI swept in and arrested thirteen men the bureau accused of plotting to abduct Michigan governor Gretchen Whitmer.[5]

Only a few months earlier, in late April, gun-toting militiamen had stormed the Michigan statehouse to protest the lockdown. Police and capitol staff fought to keep them back, but the protest raged on for hours. Hardly any of the armed demonstrators wore masks, media reports noted at the time. "Let us in! Let us in!" they chanted. Others chanted anti-government slogans and compared Whitmer to Hitler. Some of the Democratic lawmakers inside the building put on bulletproof vests, fearing the worst. The Republican state legislators, meanwhile, effectively attempted to meet the armed demonstrators' demands, refusing the sign off on the extension of the state's coronavirus-related emergency measures. "The governor, unfazed, responded with orders stating that an emergency still exists, while declaring new 28-day states of emergency and disaster," *The Guardian* reported.[6]

But in October, the feds had moved in on an even more disturbing show of defiance to the lockdown. Calling themselves the Wolverine Watchmen, these thirteen men had held training exercises, recruited widely, and been on the hunt for Whitmer's home address since April, not long before the raid on the state capitol building, according to court documents. The men had possibly planned to kill the governor, authorities said. Later, they allegedly intended to stage an armed takeover of the capitol and execute politicians on live television over the course of several weeks.[7]

Meanwhile, south of the border, migrants were still braving the journey, despite the coronavirus and the often dangerous and unhealthy conditions they had to endure en route to the United States. By the outset of October 2020, more than three-thousand people had gone over the border from Honduras into Guatemala, according to Guatemalan authorities, and were headed toward the US-Mexico border. But Mexican authorities, working in tandem with the US, had deployed the country's national guard to the frontier to head them off.[8]

Only a year earlier, Trump had reportedly suggested a slate of border-security proposals that stood out as bizarre even for him. In private conversations with White House staffers, the president had allegedly floated the idea of building a moat on the US-Mexico border. According to *The New York Times*, he had asked aides to find out how much it would cost to build a trench, fill it with water, and then stock it with alligators or snakes. "He wanted the wall electrified, with spikes on top that could pierce human flesh," the *Times* reported. "After publicly suggesting that soldiers shoot migrants if they threw rocks, the president backed off when his staff told him that was illegal. But later in a meeting, aides recalled, he suggested that they shoot migrants in the legs to slow them down. That's not allowed either, they told him."[9] (Trump dismissed the report as a fabrication, saying that he was indeed "tough" on immigration but that the article was "fake news.")[10]

As COVID-19 ravaged much of the world, apprehensions at the border had plummeted in 2020. During that fiscal year, which ended in September 2020, authorities had reported a little more than four hundred thousand people apprehended, less than half of the total number of people apprehended the previous fiscal year.[11] There was no doubt that the pandemic had temporarily slowed migration to what was comparably a trickle, but that didn't stop Trump and his administration from playing up the supposed threat ahead of the November presidential election. But throughout October, the month before the vote, arrests on the southern border spiked yet again. Border authorities arrested or detained more than sixty-nine thousand people that month, a number that marked the highest October tally in fifteen years, according to *The Washington Post*.[12] With more than four-hundred miles of walls and barriers built on the border, with Mexico and other countries trying to block migrants, and with a pandemic gripping the world, the Trump administration still couldn't make good on its promise to seal the frontier.

The week of the election, we were pushing westward, whooshing past saguaro-spotted hills and heading toward the outskirts of Three Points, a census-designated community located around forty minutes from Tucson. Joel Smith of Humane Borders was driving, and his big white pickup rattled whenever it hit rough patches of highway. Few cars were on the road, but every now and then a Border Patrol pickup blasted past us. Joel needed to check on his water barrels—a couple of months had passed since Meyer had vandalized any, but Joel needed to be sure. He pulled to the side of the highway, hopped out, and unlocked the padlock on a gate. CITY OF TUCSON PROPERTY, a sign read. "I've got the keys," Smith said, climbing back behind the steering wheel.

Smith and Humane Borders had been dealing with Meyer and Veterans on Patrol for more than two and a half years. Meyer had knifed, drained, and stolen dozens of barrels upon which many migrants making the journey depended for water. Who knew how many? How much damage the vigilantes had done, I wanted to know. Smith guessed that Meyer and his crew had cost the humanitarian aid group around $5,000 altogether.

The dirt path sliced in curves through the desert, mesquite trees lashing the truck all the way. Scrubs blanketed the flat desert land. Jackrabbits dashed away as the pickup advanced, and a hawk perched on a tree branch off to the side, watching. The sun had just come up, casting a pale glaze across the terrain. Around a half mile ahead and high up in the air, the breeze shivered through a blue flag. Smith placed his blue flags on thirty-foot poles so that migrants could spot them from far off. He called it the "law of attraction." This water station sat around twenty-seven miles from the border. Traveling the distance took less than a half hour by car, but it could take migrants several days to pass on foot. At the base of the pole was a fifty-five-gallon blue barrel, propped up on cinder blocks. "I think Meyer has an idea of where this station is, but he hasn't been able to reach it yet," he said.

Out of the truck, Smith flipped the spigot on the water barrel and did a taste test. When they weren't intentionally drained, he needed to refill his water stations once every six weeks in the summer, once every nine weeks during the winter. He let water fill up his cupped hands and then rinsed off his face. On the outside of his forearm, a tattoo of a blue flag on a pole peeked out from under his rolled-up sleeves. Since Meyer and VOP had targeted the water drops in Three Points, Joel had started moving them around every now and then. In his videos and on social media outlets, Meyer had claimed that the water stations presented a danger to children in the area—the local school was less than two miles away. But even closer were a Border Patrol checkpoint and another Border Patrol substation, and Smith had long since acquired permission to use the land for water stations. "There's nothing secretive or sensitive about this," he said. "Border Patrols know, and the City of Tucson gave us permission to be here."

Back in the truck, we headed toward the border. Rugged desert sprawled out for miles on either side of the border, and migrants crossing the frontier often drank from the wells and water tanks Smith and his organization had placed around Pima County. Humane Borders maintained dozens of water stations in some of the remote stretches of the desert. But a newly planted sign along our path appeared, with a warning. RESTRICTED ACCESS, it said. A construction crew had closed off the area. A couple hundred yards south stood the pipe fence on the border. A few miles east, the workers were busy expanding the wall; a few miles west, the same.

With Trump still in office until January 19, construction was moving ahead at a breakneck pace. Pickup trucks full of workers bounced down the access road, shooting up a spray of dust behind them. The sound of jackhammers drilling the earth somewhere far off traveled our way. As we pulled back onto Sasabe Road and set out to check another water station, a lorry carrying large slabs of concrete rolled by, whizzing past the one-story elementary school; the drooping double-wides; and a handful of unhappy homes, all boarded-up and abandoned. Every now and then, a white-and-green Border Patrol truck flicked past us, booming back and forth to the border.

As the operations manager at Humane Borders, Smith had worked in the southern Arizona borderlands for more than a decade. At fifty-seven, he'd had a busy life. His father was in the military, and he lived in Europe for a stint as child. He later served in the US Marine Corps ("during peacetime," he says). Those days, he had two adult children and put in a couple of shifts at a warehouse on weekends. But during the week, he kept busy at the nonprofit, checking the water stations all over the desert and managing a team of volunteers. I wanted to know why he got involved with humanitarian work. "I'm an old-fashioned guy," he told me. "When someone needs help, I want to help."

Using data from county medical examiner's offices, Humane Borders also maintained and regularly updated a map of deaths along Arizona's four-hundred miles of border with Mexico. Red dots represented spots where the remains of migrants had been found—and the map was blanketed with clusters of red dots, some of them on top of each other. The dead were described as "fully fleshed," "decomposed," and having undergone "complete skeletization," among other sordid descriptions. Occasionally, the search teams found "mummified" bodies. The known causes of death included everything from blunt-force trauma to gunshot wounds, hyperthermia to dehydration. Altogether, Humane Borders had documented nearly two hundred so far that year, putting 2020 on track to be the deadliest of the last seven years. How many dead bodies and skeletal remains were still out there? Impossible to say.

After all that time, Smith had never filed for an injunction against Meyer. "Anything that gets Meyer in court can set him off," he said. "We consulted a lawyer and felt we'd just be feeding his vanity . . . He'd make claims and try to establish more credibility with that. That's the sad part. I'd just like to go up to him and just drop a bowling ball on his foot."

VOP had lost their Facebook page and their Twitter page over the summer, when the social media networks cracked down on accounts that spread conspiracy theories. Smith hoped his audience would continue dwindling. The humanitarian had years earlier registered the group's name as his own, hoping to use it as a bargaining chip, but his intention to negotiate with Meyer, to hand over the name in exchange for peace, got him nowhere. "I discovered you can't negotiate with a psychopath," he told me. "That was my bad—I underestimated him entirely. I thought he was halfway sane."

For his part, Smith wanted only for VOP to leave him and his humanitarian volunteers alone. Years of harassment had worn him down, he explained, and Meyer had never stayed away for long. We rolled past the Three Points Veterans Memorial Park, and Smith brought up a video Meyer had recently posted online. "Meyer had some kind of video of him walking around that park saying there were illegals everywhere," he said. "It's easy to make these wild claims, you know. He doesn't give out facts."

In recent months, VOP had set up shop in the area, patrolling the desert trails and running a homeless camp behind a local convenience store. Every now and then, they vandalized Humane Borders's water stations, but that no longer surprised Smith. It had become a part of the job, checking on the water stations and repairing them when necessary. While most militia and vigilante groups had stopped harassing Humane Borders, VOP continued without pause. When Barack Obama was still president, the vandalism "came in cycles," he explained.

Smith believed that Tim Foley and Arizona Border Recon had once vandalized the water stations, but that they had since quit. "There will be two years and a station will be okay," he said, "and then all of a sudden" someone would knife a barrel. "It's human nature. Some people just want to hate."

Speaking with Smith that day, an irony hit me. Meyer, guided by QAnon conspiracy beliefs that children needed his protection, in a mangled way shared one core belief with his humanitarian nemesis: both wanted children to be safe. Smith had started his humanitarian work with the hope of saving children from dying while crossing the border. In fact, he had been inspired to action by the realization that his own children, had they been born in different circumstances, could have made the same journey seeking safety in another country. "I'm just old-fashioned that way," he said. "I don't like seeing people suffer."

The night before I went out with Joel Smith, I met Jim and Sue Chilton at their ranch, a pink terra-cotta home perched on a sparse hilltop. It was two days after Election Day, and the couple hoped Trump would pull it off despite the unfavorable numbers coming in. The Chiltons lived in a sprawling ranch home in Arivaca, a town that sat twelve miles from the border, as the crow flies. Jim, eighty-one, and his wife, Sue, moved here in 1987. They owned several large parcels of land and paid for the grazing rights to tens of thousands of acres. As I pulled my car onto their property, cows scrambled off the dirt path winding up toward their home. The sun was setting, casting a pink-and-orange glow across the brush-blanketed land.

On the way into town, I had passed a sandwich-board sign placed on the side of the road: RESIST THE WALL, STRENGTHEN THE SPIRIT, it read. But there on the Chilton's front porch, a row of signs leaning against the outside wall offered much different sentiments. One warned, IS THERE LIFE AFTER DEATH? TRESPASS AND FIND OUT. Another said, TRESPASSERS—PLEASE CARRY I.D. SO WE CAN NOTIFY NEXT OF KIN. Inside their home, a shotgun was propped against a wall near the front door.

Jim, a large man who smiled frequently, wore a bulky cowboy hat and a button-up striped shirt. Sue had a TRUMP-PENCE 2020 lapel pin on her sweatshirt. When I sat down, they placed a large framed map on the dinner table. The old map depicted a large swath of the borderlands surrounding their ranch, and they explained which parts constituted their private property and the land on which their cows grazed. Five and a half miles of the land they owned or worked touched the international border with Mexico.

Jim Chilton said his family could trace its roots back to Arizona since 1888, when his family established a ranch near Livingstone, a small ranching and farming settlement in central Arizona's Gila County that has since turned into a ghost town. He grew up ranching, went to Arizona State University and studied political science and economics, and then worked for Senator Carl Hayden, a Democrat. He went on to make his wealth working in municipal financing.

Since 1987, though, Jim and Sue had ranched the land where they now lived. On the border, they had seen people cross for years. The way they told it, the cartel's stranglehold on migration was reason enough for a wall much like the one Trump had promised to build. Sitting at their dining-room table, they recounted one story after another of Central American gang members and individuals working for the cartel crossing their land.

One Christmas Eve a couple of years earlier, they were opening gifts that night as part of a family tradition. When the doorbell rang, Jim opened the door and found a man "half-frozen and in bad shape," his wife recounted. The man hadn't eaten in three days. He had been lost in the desert, stumbling around and trying to find his way. The temperature had sunk to around twenty degrees, the wind was blowing hard, and the man wanted to know if he could sleep under one of their trees in the yard. Sue and Jim decided to let him sleep on the porch. "We put blankets and pads and pillows—a pile of blankets—a bedroll and everything else on the front porch, so the wind wasn't blowing [on him] . . . Well, he didn't freeze. The next morning we looked to see if the blankets were moving up and down. Is he alive or dead?"

They both laughed.

"He was alive, so I fixed him breakfast," she said. Jim later guided him to the Border Patrol, but he wanted to return to Mexico.

"All he wanted to do was go home," Jim chimed in. "We told him what would happen: they would take him to Tucson, he could have a shower, a hamburger or so, they'd put him on the bus and send him to Nogales and he'd have to walk across."

Over the years, the Chiltons said, they had fed hundreds of people who had crossed the border. But they had their views. They wanted the migration to stop. They wanted the border sealed.

Still, they insisted that they had no hard feelings for immigrants. "It's not the case," said Sue. "We've been broken into and seriously damaged twice by crossers."

"People brought their drugs in, dropped them, and now they're headed south and they break into the house and steal our stuff," Jim added. "Thousands and thousands of dollars' worth of stuff—cameras, computers, guns."

"Everything they can carry," Sue said. "Others have had home invasions where they were held at gunpoint. Others have been raped. All kinds of things. If things like that happen to you and your family, your view of the folks coming across starts to evolve toward the negative. It becomes [about] survival, an issue for your family."

Although the Chiltons had never experienced violence at the hands of anyone who had crossed the border, they insisted that it was a regular feature of life on the frontier. Sue spoke Spanish fluently and had for years. "I know what I'm seeing," she said, "and I know the tattoos. We've had MS-13 here. When I see that, you're dealing with a different thing than the guy we dealt with on Christmas Eve."

Over the years, as Border Patrol clamped down on who could cross at official ports of entry, people with criminal histories crossed without documents more often, usually on land like theirs, Jim and Sue said. "In many cases, these are also guys [who] can pay the cartel and they'll be high-dollar merchandise," claimed Sue.

They could tell stories for hours, and did. Rapists. Home invasions. Robberies. "That's a lot of what we get. When the president said rapists and murders and criminals . . . That's what we get coming between the borders," Sue continued.

The way things were panning out, however, Trump looked en route to lose the elections. A couple of miles from where we sat, construction crews continued to build the wall on either side of the Chiltons' ranch, moving toward each other. But if a new administration came to office, and Trump's wall froze, the wall would effectively reroute migration routes through their land.

I steered the conversation backed to the militias that the Chiltons had once welcomed on their land. The way Jim told it, the humanitarians were a mixed bag, but many of them "wanted open borders."

Some "legitimately want to help, and they come out and try to give away water and medical aid, and there are people in town here that insist there's no problem [on the border]," he said. "We are really, really concerned about the drugs coming through the ranch."

Jim argued that migration—because drugs came across at times—fueled the opioid crisis that had spread out across the country. "What's the cost?" he asked. "And the other cost— fire. We are always having fires on the ranch started by the drug packers or at least the crossers. We pay in advance for the . . . grazing rights, and here comes guys that burn up our grass that we've already paid for. It's kind of outrageous."

He seemed keen to hit every possible talking point about how much the costs added up to be, from migration jails to courts, from drug addiction epidemics to wildfires. "The cost really is horrendous," he said.

I wanted to know how a wall would stop any of that. I asked whether people would not simply find another way—over or under the wall—to enter the country. "Well, we've lived it now for over thirty years," he told me. "It hasn't been fun. This is a wonderful ranch. Cattle do really well. I never fed them a bale of hay. This land, even when the grass turns yellow, keeps its nutritional value ... so my cows get along just fine all year round. Even though it's so mountainous, it's not so hard to work."

His brother operated a ranch not too far away, in Three Points, where the land was less giving. "I guess the major point I want to make is, I'm not letting the cartel bully me out of my ranch," he said. "Lots of our rancher friends have left."

Jim continued. He told me to drive to Sasabe and see how far the wall would extend. I hadn't been there since December 2018, when the National Guard was putting up concertina wire on the barrier. But the wall they wanted wasn't just a wall. Jim said lighting, cameras, and sensors should be put out, along with access roads that traced the border. After a trip to the Middle East a few years earlier, the couple had decided the wall should resemble the Israeli separation wall in the occupied West Bank, a barrier patrolled day and night by troops and monitored by drones and surveillance cameras. "So, yes, walls work," he said, describing the wall in occupied Palestine as "beautiful."

———

A week after the elections, I drove out to Green Valley to visit humanitarian Shura Wallin. At seventy-nine, Wallin hadn't slowed down since the coronavirus pandemic hit. Along with other volunteers from the Green Valley-Sahua-rita Samaritans, she continued doing water drops in the desert, searching for remains, and making weekly trips across the border to provide humanitarian aid.

I sat on her couch for the third time in two years, wanting to know what how the border had changed over the last two years, four years, and twenty years. Wallin wore an oversized white T-shirt that read LOS HUMANITARI-os—"the humanitarians." She had just gotten back from visiting Sásabe, Sonora, the Mexican town across the border from Sasabe, Arizona. All morning, she had tended to four migrants whom Border Patrol had pushed back across the border. Since the pandemic had hit earlier that year, humanitarian work had become more challenging, but she kept at it.

For the last four years, the country had largely focused on the border, and Wallin worried that that the damage caused by Trump's border regime was "irreparable." She spoke of children who had been ripped away from their parents and locked up. "To me, that is demonic," she told me. "You have children now basically without parents, and you have parents without children."

At the same time, in more recent months, the border looked even more militarized than it had in previous years. Even throughout the pandemic, she had braved the risk of catching the coronavirus to visit Sásabe, Mexico, every Tuesday and deliver humanitarian goods to migrants stranded south of the border. As always, drug cartels were present in Sásabe, but the pandemic had forced the migrants into even more desperate straits. Housing was sparse, and the border was more difficult to pass. "It's horrendous," she said. "You can see the haunting and the despair, and it's so difficult. It's wonderful to be able to put your arm around someone and take their hand, but it is so difficult to comfort them in their hearts."

She added, "My heart breaks for them. And the thing that is so maddening about it is . . . I truly believe one of the reasons this does not change is because of the amount of money being made on the backs of people."

By then, she had been working on the border for two decades. She had no illusions about the migration crisis simply ending, and she had no hope that the incoming Biden administration would tear down the existing parts of the border wall, despite Biden's pledge to halt new construction. What had been built of the wall wouldn't come down in her lifetime, she suspected. "Maybe in your lifetime," she told me.

No doubt, change was possible. She had seen change throughout two decades of working on the border, though it was more times than not for the worse. "It's greed, the almighty dollar, which has more importance than a human life to [some] people," she said.

At the moment I sat in her home, we were both well aware of the workers hammering away on the border, part of a mad rush to build as much wall as possible before Trump's term came to an end. While the pandemic raged on, the building had never stopped. "You think of all that money and what could be done with that," she said, meaning how it could have been used to make the world a better place. But the money went to drones, helicopters, sensors, and the wall.

For Wallin, there was another, less obvious harm inflicted by the country's anti-immigrant policies. There in Green Valley, she knew that many of her neighbors had likely never seen the border, let alone truly understood the roots of the migration crisis. Her neighborhood was a largely Republican community, and despite the lack of hands-on knowledge about the border itself, there was a strong anti-migrant current running through it. She worried that many Americans, on top of keeping people out, were shutting themselves off from the world. "They need to go to the border and see the poverty, and see the conditions under which people are living and *have* to live," she said.

Still, she had something that resembled hope. Deep down, she believed people could change and could be won over. But it was the job of humanitarians and others of goodwill to educate them. "The question is: What can we do to help educate people so that they come to a point where they say, 'I had no idea?'" she said. Once people see the severity of the crisis, she hoped they would be moved to action. "What do you think you can you do to help change this?" she'd ask them. "If I do [something], and you do [something], pretty soon we have a groundswell."

In the meantime, she said, "I will do the best I can do. I will do what I can, and maybe I can get others to do the same."

———

The next day, I drove back out to Sasabe to see the wall up close again. Cruising past the Border Patrol substation, I saw migrants being led off a passenger bus and corralled into the fenced-in compound; there was barbwire all around, and signs that warned of restricted access. I pushed on, past a shuttered old saloon and a few abandoned homes with boarded-up windows and PRIVATE PROPERTY—NO TRESPASSING signs.

After parking by the post office on the side of Sasabe Road, I walked up a dirt slope leading to the border. A construction truck creaked along the access road hugging the border wall, beeping all the way. In the distance, a Border Patrol truck was parked a few yards from the fence. Workers wearing hazmat suits stood on cranes, working on the wall, fixing metal sheets to it and covering the open spaces between the slats. The wall was several feet taller than the last time I had seen it, a year earlier. Even farther down the border—where the wall had once came to a sudden stop—the access road had been expanded up into a steep mountain, carving its face and curling over its peak.

I was on private property—the owner told me I could walk there—but a pickup rolled up and skidded to a stop. As the window rolled down, I noticed a logo plastered on the door: STINGER BRIDGE & IRON. The man behind the wheel, who had a goatee and wore sunglasses, wanted to know who I was. When I told him I was a journalist, a voice came from the speakerphone of his car. "Who's he with?" the voice wanted to know.

"I'm freelance," I said. "Just taking some photos."

The man told me I couldn't go within 150 feet of the wall. "Not without permission and PPE," he said, meaning personal protective equipment against the coronavirus.

When he turned around and rode off, a Border Patrol agent eased his pickup truck along the access road, turning back toward town and passing me. Through his open window, I saw he wasn't wearing a mask or any other equipment. He watched me in his side mirror as he crept back toward the main road.

CONCLUSION
THE MARAUDERS

The red flags were already there. Throughout Trump's presidency, the militia movement had morphed from a loosely knit coalition of anti-government outfits, often with divergent ideologies, into something yet more frightening—a coalition of groups that could rally together behind a shared goal: keeping the president in office. Working toward that end, many groups and individuals in the militia movement joined the ranks of other Trump supporters, from the civic nationalists to the neo-Nazis, all of whom had gone to bat for the president over the previous four years.

On January 6, 2021, they all melded together, white nationalists and militiamen, QAnon conspiracy theorists and run-of-the-mill Republicans, outside the US Capitol building. Since the elections, Trump had tried it all. He had challenged results in the courtroom without any luck. He had insisted that Vice President Mike Pence could block the certification of the results. He had spent months inciting his supporters, spreading the fiction that the elections had been stolen and urging them to fight. Conspiracy theories that had made the rounds for years took on new urgency. A cabal of elites had made sure that Trump couldn't save the country, he insisted, and his supporters were prepared to become fighters.

That day, Congress was gathered at the Capitol to certify the electoral results. Operating on the false belief that they could prevent the transition to a Biden presidency, Trump supporters marched on the Capitol en masse: nearly a thousand individuals, many carrying MAKE AMERICA GREAT AGAIN flags, many armed. Tim Foley, the leader of Arizona Border Recon, was there. When the violence erupted and police officers pushed the mob back with tear gas, Foley alerted his Facebook following. "Just got gassed," he wrote. "But no surrender, no retreat." Likely realizing that he had posted evidence, he later deleted the status update, but Terry Sayles saved as in a screenshot.[1]

Earlier in the day, Trump had addressed his followers, urging them to "fight like hell" against the certification. Fight like hell they did, storming the Capitol building, barreling through police barricades, swinging and punching their way into the rotunda. Some hunted for lawmakers they intended to take hostage. Outside, a gallows had been erected for the legislators they considered traitors. "Hang Mike Pence," some chanted of the vice president, believing still that he could step in at any minute and prevent the certification, never mind that Pence had no such constitutional authority.[2]

Inside the building, rioters attacked Capitol police officers, paraded through the hallways—one of them carrying a Confederate flag, ransacked House Speaker Nancy Pelosi's office, and posed for photos. Militia groups like the Oath Keepers came together once again with far-right, pro-Trump outfits like the Proud Boys, both of whom were believed to have played leading roles in planning the assault. By the time the dust cleared, at least five people had died, among them Capitol police officers.[3]

The violence that day inspired some Republicans who had hardly wavered in their support for the president to rebuke Trump—although they had waited until the last two weeks of his term. The president was impeached for a second time, but like the first time, Democrats didn't have the numbers to prevent an acquittal. And so, once again, he walked away scot-free.

Around the country, federal authorities hunted down the Capitol rioters. Many faced felony charges that would land them behind bars. By late February, more than 275 people had been arrested, although nearly four times that number had participated in the Capitol invasion. They had come from states across the country—coming from New York and California, from Texas and Arizona—and had traveled back home without much trouble. But many had also livestreamed the raid, videotaping themselves breaking the law, and it didn't take long for people to start identifying the rioters. Some had apparently planned to kidnap and torture politicians. Others had been filmed carrying out brutal attacks on Capitol police officers: Luke Coffee, a small-time actor from Dallas, regularly used his Facebook to spread conspiracy theories, such as the claim that he had helped Trump by using explosives to detonate secret subways used by child sex traffickers. A January 6 video showed Coffee beating a police officer with a crutch in front of the Capitol.[4]

Others later claimed to have seen the light. They said Trump had sold them a lie, and insisted that they had only acted on the orders of the country's commander-in-chief. The North Texas realtor Jenna Ryan, who had in the past taken to Twitter to express sentiments such as "Heil Hitler,"[5] later lamented that she was facing at least four felony charges for merely doing what the president had asked of his supporters. "Not one patriot is standing up for me," Ryan told *The Washington Post.* "I'm a complete villain. I was down there based on what my president said. 'Stop the steal.' Now I see that it was all over nothing. He was just having us down there for an ego boost. I was there for him." "I bought into a lie," she added, and the lie is the lie, and it's embarrassing. I regret everything."[6]

Disavowals like Ryan's became increasingly common as authorities rounded up the rioters around the country. Whether they were sincere or not, one sentiment Ryan expressed rang true. After Biden was sworn into office, Trump, who had been booted from social media outlets for repeatedly violating their terms of service, went quiet.

But in late February, the former president appeared again, this time at the most notorious right-wing annual gathering in the country, the Conservative Political Action Conference (CPAC). Addressing the audience on the third day, Trump hinted at another run for the presidency in 2024 and claimed that "the incredible journey" was "far from being over."[7]

Trump wasted little time before he pivoted to the issue that perhaps most defined his four years in the White House. Without evidence, he accused the newly minted Biden administration of reversing the supposed gains he had made in securing the southern border. He repeated the same rhetoric he had used to whip up militias in the fall of 2018, when vigilantes flooded the border in response to the president's claim that a caravan of migrants heading northward toward the US border constituted an "invasion."

He claimed that the border wall "had an impact that nobody would have even believed," saying that his administration had "brought illegal crossings to historic lows" and that Biden had "recklessly eliminate[d] our border" and "triggered a massive flood of illegal immigration into our country, the likes of which we have never seen before."[8]

And, unsurprisingly, he gave a nod to the conspiracy theorists. "Perhaps worst of all, Joe Biden's decision to cancel border security has single-handedly launched a youth migrant crisis that is enriching child smugglers, vicious criminal cartels, and some of the most evil people on the planet," he said. "You see it every day. Just turn on the news. You see it every day."[9]

———

For their part, Michael "Screwy Louie" Meyer and his followers in Veterans on Patrol cranked up the heat. In a December 2020 YouTube video, Meyer claimed that the Pima County Sheriff's Department and Pima County Attorney Barbara LaWall had tried to "eliminate" him for supposedly removing "cartel water stations" near an elementary school. "They framed Lewis for exposing the sheriff helping cartel smugglers," a caption reads, but he insists that he was "vindicated" by the court after "6 months of arbitrary detention."[10]

The way the video tells it, Meyer left jail and sped directly to desert corridors in the southern Arizona, or what he calls "child trafficking routes." The video zooms in on a still image of a cracked cell phone screen, a phone he claimed to have taken off someone in the desert. "Coyotes, sex offenders, and criminals are being caught by VOP on a regular basis," the captions continue. Screenshots of individuals' personal Facebook pages flash on the screen, Meyer apparently insinuating that the accounts belong to smugglers, child sex traffickers, and criminals of all assortments: "Stash houses and smuggling routes are being eliminated now." Footage from trail cameras—which shows men dressed in camouflage walking through the desert at night—is accompanied by captions insisting that those who cross the border aren't asylum seekers. Of course, no one—not humanitarian groups, not officials—had claimed that everyone who crossed into the country had good intentions or intended to apply for asylum, but that didn't matter to VOP.

Near the end, the video includes an image of Meyer holding a man, ostensibly someone who crossed the frontier, by his arm. The captions say he continued to work in tandem with the Border Patrol, supposedly "compromising both smugglers and their allies."

In February 2021, Meyer posted another video, this one titled "Children Crying in the Desert."[11] No children can be heard crying in the video, but there is plenty of desert. For nearly an hour, his camera phone is shakily trained on a patch of scrub-flecked desert lands. At the beginning of the clip, an upside-down American flag beats in the wind, the afternoon bright and blue. When the sky starts to drain of daylight, the mountains are blued against the dusk. "The border communities are in distress," he says, his face not in the frame. "So many don't even see the threats. So many are helping. It's insane to see how many people have stepped up to help smuggle everyone up through here."

Meyer bangs on for a long time, talking about a string of seemingly unrelated topics. He claims that children have been raped and impregnated, that he'd seen photos of "babies with babies in their belly," a statement that defies obvious medical consensus. "These people are sick," he claims.

For months, his rhetoric had grown increasingly apocalyptic, and after a while, he informs his audience that God has chosen him. He pauses between statements, his breathing ragged. "You can judge by the fruits 'cause we do what we do with God, and without money, and without playing by their rules, we have children that we've rescued, and we have a whole lot more, I'm telling you, God's getting ready to send us to rescue," he says.

He adds that God wants people to sing and dance, but that "people are afraid to do that" because they'd end up in a mental healthcare facility or be labeled a "racist" and a "radical Christian." He continues, "I've seen the devil try to do everything to get me out of this desert."

His sermon drags on and on. In Meyer's version of reality, his work in the desert is part of a biblical-type war against Satan. Like Christ, he is leading the battle against supposedly dark forces. He likens himself to several Biblical characters. "We're surrounded by the enemy. Our entire county, our entire government, our entire state—those in authority, those in the justice system—they're all in favor of children being raped and smuggled over these mountains," he goes on. "And they're in charge."

Then he lapses into a sudden prayer, raising his voice, the rhetorical flavor more local than spiritual. "Use us, God," he pleads. "Use us to show them that they're not in charge, you do not approve of these fraudulent faith-based organizations utilizing any funds to provide any woman or child contraceptives and the morning-after pill, to assist and pay any coyote to smuggle unaccompanied children.

No, Father, they do this in your name out here. South of me is a camp that the Pima County officials protect. You know that camp, Lord. They claim to be doing your work when they don't even believe in you. Well, here we are. We give us this camp to you. We use it for your will. It is our will that you would use us to rescue these children—don't let 'em cry no more. Send us the people, send us the people we need to have to go and find every child in our area."

The video was geotagged in Three Points, and it appears likely Meyer meant the Byrd Camp, an impromptu encampment run by No More Deaths. He says it is time to "draw a line in the desert," to prevent "child crimes" on land God supposedly gave to humanity. "God, we are tired of the devil continuing to trick, distract, deceive. Even those of us, God, who know you with no doubt, who walk with no fear, he even deceives us," he says. "Don't let 'em. I rebuke him in the name of Yeshua. Satan has no authority on this land, nor does he even any authority coming onto it—ever, period."

After a while, Meyer's sermon fizzles out. True to form, he brings it full circle by insisting that he would prevent the cartels, the CIA, politicians, and federal government agencies supposedly trafficking children across the border. He vows to "remove all the filth and trash that they've done."

And then he flips the camera back to his face and asks his audience if they have any questions he can answer.

In March, the same weekend Trump claimed "dangerous predators" were storming the southern border, Meyer, Veterans on Patrol, and an allied anti-immigrant group got busy in southern Arizona, not far from Arivaca. Meyer and his crew surrounded Byrd Camp and spent hours attempting to intimidate the humanitarians who were working in the area. That same night, Meyer and other groups shared a livestream of the video on their Facebook and Parler pages, but the videos disappeared not long after.

———

In April 2021, hundreds packed into an auditorium at Rhema Bible Training College in Broken Arrow, Oklahoma, for what the organizers dubbed the Health and Freedom Conference. On the itinerary were two days of activities and speeches. The speakers included a coterie of QAnon supporters, anti-lockdown advocates, conservative Christian pastors, and far-right figures: MyPillow's Mike Lindell, the former Trump appointee and retired general Michael Flynn, Tulsa sheriff Vic Regalado, and even an actor who had starred in Mel Gibson's *The Passion of the Christ*, among others. At the end of the second day, everyone participated in a mask-burning event, a show of defiance to coronavirus-related guidelines designed to minimize exposure to the disease.[12]

When Tim Foley took the microphone, he wasn't shy about sharing his credentials in the anti-immigrant movement. Predictably, he didn't wear a suit and tie like many of the speakers had. He had been patrolling the border for twelve years, he boasted, and he knew the truth the "mainstream media" hid from the American public. He dragged up old talking points, including the tired and demonstrably false claims that women and children didn't cross the border from Mexico into southern Arizona. He blasted the Biden administration for not continuing Trump's border wall.

He also delivered a curious—and to me, unlikely—story about a phone call he supposedly received from "the cartel," though he didn't mention *which* cartel. "Two months ago I got a phone call from the cartel," he began. "Oh, they know exactly who I am, and I really don't care. But they offered me fifteen-thousand dollars a month to go away."[13]

The way Foley told it, he replied, "You know, unlike you people, I have morals. And I would have to look at myself in the mirror for the rest of my life and say, 'What did you do?' So, I turned him down. I said thanks for showing the respect, for offering that kind of money. But I asked him, 'Before we go, where did you come up with fifteen-thousand dollars?' He goes, 'That's what we pay our Border Patrol agents.'"

Foley went on to claim—without evidence—that at least a quarter of Border Patrol agents were "on the cartel take," a fact that made his "job a whole hell of a lot harder because I don't know who I can trust who's supposed to be on my side."

In typical fashion, he bragged about the supposed price that cartels had put on his head. According to Foley, "the cartel" phoned him two weeks later and said they had upped the price on his life. "If anybody needs some money," he told the crowd, "I'm up to two-hundred and fifty thousand dollars. But the only problem is you gotta take [my] head and then take it back to Mexico to prove." He then likened American politicians to drug cartels and urged his audience to "not back down."

"I don't back down," he said, raising his voice. "I never will. I will keep doing what I do. This is not for fame and fortune; it's not for me. It's for you. I do it for the country that I love. And to tie this into what we've been talking about all day long: in the twelve years I've been out there, every time I stop an illegal, or we stop a dope mule, guess what type of identification they're carrying. Voter ID cards."

The crowd broke out in laughter, but Foley tried to spin the comment into a serious point. "It's true," he said. "Guatemala, Honduras, Mexico, El Salvador—the only ID we get is voter ID cards. So, it's okay in a third-world country, but it's racist here in this country. And that shows you the insanity of what's going on in DC. Remember, we're looking for leaders. Stand up. Get off the couch. Do something, anything. *Take your country back.*"

As Foley handed off the microphone, the crowd applauded the vigilante. A host urged the crowd to donate to Arizona Border Recon and then warned that the country was on the brink of becoming a communist regime.

Later, as Foley traveled back to Arizona, he celebrated the event on Facebook and took a shot at airlines for imposing mask restrictions. "Great time in Tulsa with great people. Flight home was different story," he wrote. "[S]outhwest [A] irlines has masks nazi[s]for flight attendants. One person booted from plane. Lots of arguments. Thought fists were going fly." The following day, he doubled down. In another Facebook post, he shared a photo of a yellow star meant to signify Jews under the Nazi regime. Written on the star was a single word: UNVACCINATED.

The FBI field office in Dallas sat around ten miles north of downtown. A fence traced the perimeter of the property, and behind it were five stories of drab gray concrete and dark windows that reflected the sunlight back at you in sharp shards. Driving there, you passed the homeless encampments in empty fields and on the shoulder of highways—sometimes beneath the overpasses—all over the city. A guard checked your vehicle, made sure you have an appointment or were on a list of expected visitors, and reminded you that no cell phones are allowed inside.

I was back in Dallas. Almost two months after the January 6 riot, on March 5, the field office invited a dozen or so local reporters and television journalists to come in and hear Special Agent in Charge Matthew DeSarno's updates on domestic terrorism. It was a Friday, the afternoon charcoal and heavy, and I drove down there through the traffic-choked highways snaking the city.

After we all passed through security—no cell phones, no weapons, no GPS devices allowed—we took an elevator up to the second floor, where we sat spaced out in a conference room due to the ongoing coronavirus pandemic. DeSarno arrived around 2:30 p.m.

He kicked off by speaking of the FBI's mission, making the necessary prefaces: The bureau didn't police ideology; the bureau respected everyone's constitutional rights; the bureau valued transparency and a line of communication with the press. When he got around to speaking of the January 6 riot, he had new numbers. The Dallas field office had thus far arrested seventeen alleged Capitol insurrectionists, the largest number of any of the fifty-six field offices dotting the country. He said violent extremism was "metastasizing" around the nation. Unlike the days of Waco, Ruby Ridge, and the Oklahoma City bombing, hard-line extremists who now "are radicalized are not on the fringes of society": "We're talking about parts of the mainstream of society that have been radicalized to the point where they have mobilized to commit acts of violence or commit federal crimes in furtherance of their own ideology."

DeSarno had peppered-gray hair and wore a suit and tie. As he spoke, he flipped through a thick binder of papers sat on the table in front of him. He said investigating domestic terrorism investigations stood out among the most challenging investigative programs the bureau had. Less than a month prior, his agents had nabbed a twenty-year-old neo-Nazi on a federal gun charge in nearby Grand Prairie: Christian Mackey, a member of Iron Youth, had attempted to sell a rifle to an undercover agent and wound up in cuffs. The same day, the FBI field office in San Antonio arrested another Iron Youth member who had tried to purchase a machine gun from an undercover agent.

What kept DeSarno up at night wasn't the possibility of another incident like the Capitol riot. He seemed to feel the crackdown would deter another such event. Rather, what he lost sleep over was the idea of an individual not necessarily plugged into any network of extremists who would carry out a mass shooting or slap together homemade bombs. "The number-one terrorism threat is a lone actor, radicalized here in the United States, radicalized to a point where they are mobilized to violence, looking to attack soft targets with either crude or readily available weapons," he said. DeSarno equated far-right extremists with violent Islamists like al-Qaeda and the Islamic State in Iraq and Syria (ISIS). But then he went on to lump leftists—anarchists and anti-fascists—in with the rest of the lot. "What we've seen generally is that [the] continuum is no longer a left and right continuum but has become a sphere, an arc of a continuum where down here at the bottom, you've got people who really have the same goals for step one and different goals for step two, with step one being the breaking down or destroying of democratic institutions," he said. "That's something both antifa and the Proud Boys agree should happen—that we've gotta get rid of what we got right now."

The way DeSarno told it, leftists, anarchists, white nationalists, and militiamen, among others, were all the same: "anti-government extremists." "Anarchist," to the special agent in charge, was a term that applied equally to the Oath Keepers and antifa.

For years, federal and local law enforcement agencies had clamped down on leftists, environmentalists, and Muslims, but there were few out there who believed the nation's security forces had taken the threat of far-right groups and militia outfits seriously. Around an hour and a half southeast of the FBI field office, in Hood County, the Oath Keepers militia had spent years infiltrating local law enforcement and government.[14] In fact, Hood County Constable John D. Shirley had penned an op-ed in the local *Hood County Today* newspaper explaining why he had joined the militia. "I've been a member of Oath Keepers for over a decade and have held multiple leadership positions at both the State and National levels, and in that time I've seen the multiple waves of attacks by the media and progressive NGOs (such as the SPLC)," Shirley wrote, referring to the Southern Poverty Law Center, a frequent target of right-wing hate. The constable concluded his ode to the militia: "If you think you have a problem with the Oath Keepers, what you actually have a problem with is the U.S. Constitution."[15]

But the cozy relationship between many law enforcement agencies and radical right-wing groups—including militias—didn't come up that day at the FBI field office. His agents were busy hunting down the Capitol rioters, people who Trump had mobilized, encouraged, and celebrated, though their ideologies didn't make an appearance in his presentation. The FBI had received more than two hundred thousand tips nationwide, and the Dallas team was opening new investigations each week. "The real challenge is the volume," he said. "Many of you have covered some of the folks who we've arrested, and they, as you know, represent the mainstream of society in a lot of ways."

DeSarno said that bureau was implementing the same strategy the country's security apparatuses used to prevent international terrorist attacks. "If someone had mobilized to the point where they were inside the Capitol, or they were assaulting a Capitol police officer, or they were damaging that building on that day, we want to move quickly with whatever charges we can prove now to get them in custody," he said.

———

Nearly a thousand miles away in Arivaca, no one had arrested Tim Foley. Since returning from Washington, DC, he had deleted his status updates about being inside the Capitol building. All around the country, federal authorities had swept up January 6 rioters who posted selfies and videos inside the building during the unrest. Meanwhile, Foley continued what appeared to be his normal routine. On his Facebook and the militia's Facebook, he railed against President Joe Biden, demonized immigrants, and warned his followers of the supposed socialism soaking into the nation's institutions. Even hate becomes routine.

Around the same time DeSarno was speaking to reporters in Dallas, Foley took to the Arizona Border Recon Facebook page and shared a news article about newly arrived asylum seekers in southern Arizona. The article, published by a local newspaper, said that Biden's border policies had set in, and that busloads of migrants had started showing up in Tucson.[16] "And so it begins," wrote Foley, "the calm before the storm in Tucson."

Whether or not by "storm" he meant the arrival of migrants, it struck me, although perhaps less likely, that "storm" could just as well apply to his own plans, the ideas he now had in mind to stop migrants from crossing the border. Foley didn't say one way or another. But the first comment beneath the post, written by one of Arizona Border Recon's followers, seemed to suggest an answer: "Chase them back to the border," it read. "Make them unwelcome."

———

In our minds, the word "marauder" draws up images of intruders on horseback, invading communities and snatching up whatever they see fit to steal, raiding, looting, and robbing. In the American lexicon, the term also brings to mind certain myths. Native Americans, many of us were taught, terrorized settler communities with brutal, and often deadly, raids on innocent civilians. In more recent iterations of this idea, migrants and foreigners intrude, slipping over the border and usurping what belongs to us.

But the entire notion is bankrupt. For those living in communities like Arivaca, people have crossed the border and passed through town for decades, usually without incident. In the two years I spent visiting the community, most residents, including those with conservative views on immigration, rarely blamed the migrants themselves for problems in the borderlands. But even most of the right-leaning townspeople I spoke with saw the militias as outsiders who stirred up trouble more than anything else. They often came from hundreds, sometimes thousands, of miles away, armed to the teeth with weapons, and disrupted the very quiet most people moved to the town to find.

The way the militiamen see it, they are welcomed by those whose welcome matters most. Border Patrol may try and distance themselves from the newcomers, but there's no doubt that sympathetic agents reside in their ranks. At the end of the day, after all, the militiamen and the Border Patrol agents have overlapping goals: keeping migrants south of the border, or catching them as soon as they cross onto American soil. But even if Border Patrol agents uniformly detested the militias, even if every Arivacan took to the streets and protested the militiamen's presence in town, it's hard to imagine Tim Foley or Michael Lewis Arthur Meyer abandoning course. The communities they've marauded have told them to go home—they've protested, they've boycotted, they've appealed to law enforcement—and neither Foley nor Meyer, nor any of the vigilante groups, have packed up and left.

It's impossible to consider Arivaca's story—or many like it across the southern border—without considering decades of westerns, films, and novels that have shaped our views of the American Southwest and the borderlands. Parlaying a white supremacist narrative, these adventures have "little to do with the real nineteenth-century frontier life," as the film critic Philip French notes in his monograph *Westerns*. Rather, "the rituals are enacted [in these movies]in a timeless world where it is always high noon in some dusty cow town west of St. Louis. Rather like . . . the Never-Never Land of . . . *Peter Pan*, populated by children who refuse to grow-up, fugitives from the urban nursery, marauding Indians and menacing bands of pirates."[17]

To this day, many of us see the frontier as lawless.

The border is everywhere. Barbwire. Walls. Protests. Guards. Guns. Surveillance drones. Checkpoints. Interrogations, arrests, and deportations. Tear gas, flash bangs, and bullets. Borders are walled, fenced, mountainous, or made of water. Borders are guarded, porous, populated, desolate, or hard to reach. Borders are easy to cross or nearly impossible to surpass.

Migration stretches back as long as human history. For as long as people have populated the earth, they have moved from one place to the next. And for as long as they have moved from one place to the next, others have tried to keep them out. Walls encircled Jericho, the biblical city in present-day Palestine, as far back as the tenth millennium B.C., as they did in most cities in ancient antiquity. Fearing invasion by outsiders—Goths, Huns, Mongols—Mesopotamians erected the first border walls in the late 2000s B.C., according to the historian David Frye.[18]

Walls can be scaled or tunneled under. Going over a wall or beneath it doesn't make one a marauder. But flooding a community, armed and angry, seems to fit the definition quite well. When the militias showed up in Arivaca, they were outsiders just as much as, if not more than, the people passing through. They set up camp on land that was once Indigenous, that was later Mexican, and that was never, beyond virtue of having American citizenship, theirs. They claimed stake in a history that they could only adopt. They rode into town in trucks rather than on horseback. They claimed the community as their own. They promised to put a stop to a situation with consequences they had never had to endure. Some may not have seen them as a problem. Some, like the Chiltons, welcomed them.

ACKNOWLEDGMENTS

I wish to thank the entire team at Melville House who contributed to this book entering the world, including Dennis Johnson, Valerie Merians, and their copyeditor Amanda Gersten. To my editor, Carl Bromley, thank you for the editorial advice and your patience. Thanks, too, to the professors who gave me helpful feedback on several chapters of this book while I was attending the University of Nebraska-Omaha's creative writing MFA program: Kate Gale, Kevin Clouther, and Patricia Lear, among others. I'm grateful to the many journalists who have covered the far right in the borderlands, especially David Neiwert for his invaluable book on Arivaca, *And Hell Followed with Her*. Many thanks to the reporters, researchers and writers around the country who have kept shining a light on the far right and militias: Jason Wilson, Shane Burley, Leah Sottile, Tay Wiles, and Nick Martin, to name a few. I appreciate the mountains of advice friends and colleagues gave me on everything from subject material to sentences, chief among them Laurin-Whitney Gottbrath. I also want to record my gratitude to my family, especially my mother. I'll never be able to repay Dr. Nancy Stockdale for all her support: thank you, Nancy. Finally, this book would have been impossible had the people who spoke to me not been willing to share their stories.

NOTES

NOTES TO THE INTRODUCTION

1   Emi Suzuki," Newly Released Data Show Refugee Numbers at Record Levels," *World Bank Blogs*, June 19, 2019, https://blogs. worldbank.org/opendata/newly-released-data-show-refugee-numbers-record-levels.

2   Morgan Loew, "Border Town Takes Stand Against Militias," *AZFamily.com* (CBS 5), October 25, 2018, https://www.azfamily. com/news/investigations/cbs_5_investigates/border-town-takes-stand-against-militias/article_fb0eb244-d7ce-11e8-99fa-93e489605fd4.html.

3   Federal Bureau of Investigation, "Justice in Kansas," FBI. gov, April 12, 2019, https://www.fbi.gov/news/stories/three-sentenced-in-plot-to-bomb-somali-immigrants-041219.

4   "Kansas Militia Men Blame Trump Rhetoric for Mosque Attack Plan," Reuters, October 30, 2018, https://www.reuters.com/ article/us-kansas-crime-somalia/kansas-militia-men-blame-trump-rhetoric-for-mosque-attack-plan-idUSKCN1N5O0O.

5   "Kansas Militia Men Blame Trump Rhetoric for Mosque Attack Plan."

6   "Kansas Militia Men Blame Trump Rhetoric for Mosque Attack Plan."

NOTES TO CHAPTER 1

1   Curt Prendergast, "Armed Vigilantes Bring Unease to Arizona Border Town Haunted by Killing of Girl, Dad," *Arizona Daily Star* (Tucson.com), October 8, 2018, https://tucson.com/ news/local/armed-vigilantes-bring-unease-to-arizona-border-town-haunted-by/article_338c98ba-1850-5540-8e6a-571351366b70.html.

2   Taylor W. Anderson, "The Utah Gun Exchange Is Following the Parkland Students Around the Country to Combat Their Call for More Gun Laws," *The Salt Lake Tribune*, July 10, 2018, https://www.sltrib.com/news/politics/2018/07/10/utah-gun-exchange-is/.

3   BuildTheWallTv, "Jim & Sue Chilton Unedited and Uncut – BuildTheWallTV," YouTube video, 59:32, September 20, 2018, https://www.youtube.com/watch?v=O4Qix1_PPWA.

NOTES TO CHAPTER 2

1   John Weiss Forney, *Anecdotes of Public Men* (Volume 1), Los Angeles: Hard Press Publishing, January 28, 2013, pg. 130.

2   John C. Forman, *Lewis C. Levin: Portrait of an American Demagogue* (Cincinnati: American Jewish Archives, 1960).

3   Sean Wilentz, *Chants Democratic: New York City and the Rise of the American Working Class, 1788–1850* (Oxford University Press, 1984),315–325.

4   All quotes from Perry are drawn from Historical Society of Pennsylvania, "Full and Complete Account of the Late Philadelphia Riots," *A Full and Complete Account of the Late Awful Riots in Philadelphia* (Philadelphia, PA: John B. Perry, 1844), https://hsp.org/sites/default/files/legacy_files/migrated/fullaccountofkensingtoncompletefinal.pdf.

5   Brendan Spiegel, "The Donald Trump of the 1940s," *Narratively*, August 1, 2016, https://narratively.com/the-donald-trump-of-the-1840s/.

6   Spiegel, "The Donald Trump of the 1940s."

7   Kurt F. Stone, "Lewis Charles Levin (1809–1860), Served 1845–1851," in *The Jews of Capitol Hill: A Compendium of Jewish Congressional Members* (Lanham, MD: Scarecrow Press), 10.

8   Brendan Spiegel, "Donald Trump of the 1940s."

9   Brendan Spiegel, "Donald Trump of the 1940s."

10   James McPherson, *Battle Cry of Freedom: The Civil War Era* (Oxford University Press, 1988), 130.

11   Brendan Spiegel, "Donald Trump of the 1940s."

12   John Hancock Lee, *The Origin and Progress of the American Party in Politics: Embracing a Complete History of the Philadelphia Riots in May and July, 1944. With a Full Description of the Great American Procession of July Fourth and a Refutation of the Arguments Founded on*, Los Angeles: Hard Press Publishing, August 1, 2012, pg. 14.

13   Alan Taylor, *American Republics: A Continental History of the United States, 1783–1850* (New York: W.W. Norton and Co., 2021), 240.

14   Streets of Washington, "The Election Day riots of 1857, driven by religious intolerance," December 15, 2015, http://www.streetsofwashington.com/2015/12/the-election-day-riot-of-1857-driven-by.html.

15   Ron Grossman, "Chicago's lager beer riot proved immigrants' power," *Chicago Tribune*, September 25, 2015, https://www.chicagotribune.com/history/ct-know-nothing-party-lager-beer-riot-per-flashback-jm-20150925-story.html.

16   Ancient Order of Hibernians, Louisville, Kentucky, "Bloody Monday Memorial: About Bloody Monday," https://www.louisvilleirish.com/bloody-monday-memorial/.

17   "The Riots in Louisville" (from the *Louisville Journal*), *The New York Times*, August 7, 1855, https://timesmachine.nytimes.com/timesmachine/1855/08/10/75802029.pdf?pdf_redirect=true&ip=0.

18   Ancient Order of Hibernians, "Bloody Monday Memorial."

19   Annalisa Merelli, "A History of American Anti-Immigrant Bias, Starting with Benjamin Franklin's Hatred of the Germans," *Quartz*, February 12, 2017, https://qz.com/904933/a-history-of-american-anti-immigrant-bias-starting-with-benjamin-franklins-hatred-of-the-germans/.

20   Marian L. Smith, "Race, Nationality, and Reality: INS Administration of Racial Provisions in U.S. Immigration and Nationality Law Since 1898," Prologue 34, no. 2 (Summer 2002), Archives.gov, https://www.archives.gov/publications/prologue/2002/summer/immigration-law-1.html.

21   PBS: American Experience, "Chinese Immigrants and the Gold Rush," https://www.pbs.org/wgbh/americanexperience/features/goldrush-chinese-immigrants/.

22   ImmigrationHistory.org (The Immigration and Ethnic History Society), "People v. Hall (1854)," https://immigrationhistory.org/item/people-v-hall/.

23   Wendy Rouse, "People v. Hall," in *Defining Documents: Manifest Destiny and the New Nation (1803–1860)* (Ipswich, MA: Salem Press/EBSCO Publishing, 2013), 194.

24   Kelly Wallace, "Forgotten Los Angeles History: The Chinese Massacre of 1871," Los Angeles Public Library (blog), May 19, 2017, https://www.lapl.org/collections-resources/blogs/lapl/chinese-massacre-1871.

25   Reynaldo Leanos Jr., "This Underground Railroad Took Slaves to Freedom In Mexico," *GBH News*, March 31, 2017, https://www.wgbh.org/news/2017/03/31/underground-railroad-took-slaves-freedom-mexico.

26   Russell Contreras, "AP Explains: Militias have patrolled US border for decades," Associated Press, May 12, 2019, https://apnews.com/article/immigration-new-mexico-north-america-us-news-ap-top-news-12dd5d7564304f35860efe3a64fc6f93.

27   Alexander Berkman, *The Bolshevik Myth* (New York: Boni and Liveright, 1925), available at Anarchy Archives, http://dwardmac.pitzer.edu/Anarchist_Archives/bright/berkman/bmyth/bmch1.html.

28   Jewish Women's Archive, "Deportation of Emma Goldman as a Radical 'Alien,'" https://jwa.org/thisweek/dec/21/1919/emma-goldman.

29   Emma Goldman, "Deportation to Russia," in *My Disillusionment in Russia* (New York: Doubleday, Page & Company, 1923), available at the Marxists.org Emma Goldman Reference Archive, https://www.marxists.org/reference/archive/goldman/works/1920s/disillusionment/ch01.htm.

30   Paul A. Offit, "The Loathsome American Book that Inspired Hitler," *Daily Beast*, August 26, 2017, https://www.thedailybeast.com/the-loathsome-american-book-that-inspired-hitler.

31   Becky Little, "The U.S. Deported a Million of Its Own Citizens to Mexico During the Great Depression," *History*, July 12, 2019, https://www.history.com/news/great-depression-repatriation-drives-mexico-deportation.

32   United States Holocaust Memorial Museum, "How Many Refugees Came to the United States from 1933-1945?," https://exhibitions.ushmm.org/americans-and-the-holocaust/how-many-refugees-came-to-the-united-states-from-1933-1945.

33 Daniel A. Gross, "The U.S. Government Turned Away Thousands of Jewish Refugees, Fearing That They Were Nazi Spies," *Smithsonian Magazine*, November 18, 2015, https://www.smithsonianmag.com/history/us-government-turned-away-thousands-jewish-refugees-fearing-they-were-nazi-spies-180957324/.

34 Kathleen Belew, *Bring the War Home* (Cambridge, MA: Harvard University Press, 2018), 38.

35 Southern Poverty Law Center, "Louis Beam," https://www.splcenter.org/fighting-hate/extremist-files/individual/louis-beam.

36 Southern Poverty Law Center, "Louis Beam."

37 Vanda Felbab-Brown and Elisa Noro, "What Border Vigilantes Taught US Right-Wing Armed Groups," Brookings Institute, March 12, 2021, https://www.brookings.edu/articles/what-border-vigilantes-taught-us-right-wing-armed-groups/.

NOTES TO CHAPTER 3

1 Rick Anderson, "How a Teen Prostitute and Beautician Morphed into a Minuteman American Defense Leader and Alleged Killer," *Phoenix New Times*, July 16, 2009, https://www.phoenixnewtimes.com/news/how-a-teen-prostitute-and-beautician-morphed-into-a-minuteman-american-defense-leader-and-alleged-killer-6432818.

2 Rick Anderson, "Teen Prostitute and Beautician."

3 Megan Cassidy, "Ex-Minuteman Chris Simcox sentenced to 19.5 years in child sex-abuse case," AZCentral.com, July 11, 2016, https://www.azcentral.com/story/news/local/phoenix/2016/07/11/chris-simcox-sentenced-child-sex-abuse/86948200/.

4 David Holthouse, "Nativist leader arrested for double murder," Southern Poverty Law Center, June 15, 2009, https://www.splcenter.org/hatewatch/2009/06/15/nativist-leader-arrested-double-murder.

5 Scott North, "No boundaries: Shawna Forde and the Minutemen movement," HeraldNet, October 25, 2009, https://www.heraldnet.com/news/no-boundaries-shawna-forde-minutemen-movement/.

6   Scott North, "No boundaries: Shawna Forde and the Minutemen movement."

7   Scott North, "Forde's co-defendant has a long, disturbing history," HeraldNet, February 1, 2011, https://www.heraldnet. com/news/fordes-co-defendant-has-long-disturbing-history/.

8   State v. Forde, Case No. CR–11–0043–AP, Supreme Court of Arizona, January 17, 2014, https://caselaw.findlaw.com/az-supreme-court/1655105.html.

9   David Neiwert, *And Hell Followed With Her: Crossing the Dark Side of the American Border*, Nation Books, March 26, 2013, pg. 71.

10   Tim Steller, "Home Invasion: How Map Destroyed by FBI Could have Saved Little Girl," *Arizona Daily Star* (Tucson.com), February 25, 2016, https://tucson.com/news/local/columnists/ steller/home-invasion-how-map-destroyed-by-fbi-could-have-saved/article_80500b2d-a080-5c97-a163-d1634364353f.html.

11   David Neiwert, *And Hell Followed with Her*, pg. 8.

12   Neiwert, *And Hell Followed With Her*, pg 55.

13   State v. Forde.

14   David Neiwert, "Oin Oakstar, 43, Key Figure in Shawna Forde Trial, Found Dead in Homeless Encampment," *Hatewatch* (blog), Southern Poverty Law Center, October 10, 2014, https://www. splcenter.org/hatewatch/2014/10/10/oin-oakstar-43-key-figure-shawna-forde-trial-found-dead-homeless-encampment.

15   State v. Forde.

16   Neiwert, *And Hell Followed With Her*, pg 12.

17   All quotes from the 911 call are drawn from the recording available on YouTube: True Crime Review, "Gina Gonzalez Calls 911 to Report Murder of Her Husband and Daughter by Shawna Forde and Co," 20:01, December 9, 2016, https://www.youtube. com/watch?v=-BJP89OoPEA.

18   Neiwert, *And Hell Followed With Her*, pg. 3.

19   State v. Forde.

20   Tim Steller, "Suit: FBI Failed to Stop Arivaca Deaths," Arizona Daily Star (Tucson.com), June 1, 2012, updated July 8, 2014, https://tucson.com/news/local/crime/suit-fbi-failed-to-stop-arivaca-deaths/article_8ae54c50-c5da-598e-81cd-4c5aeb80c644.html.

21   Daniel Newhauser, "Official: Arivaca Suspect Confessed
      to Murders," *Nogales International*, July 13, 2009, updated
      November 21, 2012, https://www.nogalesinternational.com/
      santa_cruz_valley_sun/news/official-arivaca-suspect-
      confessed-to-murders/article_a49cb9ca-d6df-53bf-ab92-
      467d266318f7.html.

22   Daniel Newhauser and Dan Shearer, "3 Suspects Arrested
      in Arivaca Murders," *Nogales International*, June 15, 2009,
      https://www.nogalesinternational.com/news/suspects-
      arrested-in-arivaca-murders/article_ef91ead5-615a-50d4-b102-
      f7dd087ec801.html.

23   "Shawna Forde's Alleged Conspirator Is Now Charged in 1997
      East Wenatchee Killing," *HeraldNet* (Everett), July 31, 2009,
      https://www.heraldnet.com/news/shawna-fordes-alleged-
      conspirator-is-now-charged-in-1997-east-wenatchee-killing/.

24   Southern Poverty Law Center, "Active 'Patriot' Groups in
      the United States in 2011," *Intelligence Report*, March 8,
      2012, https://www.splcenter.org/fighting-hate/intelligence-
      report/2012/active-%E2%80%98patriot%E2%80%99-groups-
      united-states-2011.

25   Kim Smith, "Lawsuit in Deadly Arivaca Home Invasion
      Dismissed," *Arizona Daily Star* (Tucson.com), February 4, 2013,
      updated February 11, 2020, https://tucson.com/news/local/
      crime/lawsuit-in-deadly-arivaca-home-invasion-dismissed/
      article_17821f90-6f13-11e2-ba23-0019bb2963f4.html.

NOTES TO CHAPTER 4

1   Nick R. Martin, "Extremists go to 'war' in the Arizona
      desert," Talking Points Memo, March 20, 2012, https://
      talkingpointsmemo.com/muckraker/extremists-go-to-war-in-
      the-arizona-desert.

2   Shannon Crawford, Lauren Effron, and Neal Karlinsky, "Out
      on Patrol with Heavily Armed Civilian Vigilantes on Arizona's
      Border with Mexico," *ABC News*, February 1, 2017, https://
      abcnews.go.com/US/patrol-heavily-armed-civilian-vigilantes-
      arizonas-border-mexico/story?id=45201990.

3   Tim Steller, "Border Militiaman Under Lawmen's Spotlight,"
     Arizona Daily Star (Tucson.com), June 9, 2012, updated July 8,
     2014, https://tucson.com/news/local/crime/border-militiaman-
     under-lawmen-s-spotlight/article_60031e06-1cb3-5183-bfc6-
     dad9b8feadcb.html.

4   Daniel Gonzalez, "Sasabe border outpost one of quietest in U.S.,"
     KOLD 13 via *The Arizona Republic*, November 27, 2011, https://
     www.kold.com/story/16130522/sasabe-border-outpost-one-of-
     quietest-in-nation/.

5   U.S. Fish and Wildlife Service, "Media advisory: Border
     refuge not closed," https://www.fws.gov/southwest/docs/
     MediaAdvisory.BorderRefugeOpen.62010.pdf.

6   Fernanda Santos, "At the Southern Border, a Do-It-Yourself Tack
     on Security," *The New York Times*, December 21, 2016, https://
     www.nytimes.com/2016/12/21/us/at-the-southern-border-a-do-
     it-yourself-tack-on-security.html.

7   Laura Mallonee, "On a Mission with the Men of Arizona
     Border Recon," *Wired*, September 23, 2015, https://www.wired.
     com/2015/09/mission-men-arizona-border-recon/.

8   Peter Holley, "These Armed Civilians Are Patrolling the Border
     to Keep ISIS out of America," *The Washington Post*, November
     25, 2015, https://www.washingtonpost.com/news/morning-mix/
     wp/2015/11/25/these-armed-civilians-are-patrolling-the-border-
     to-keep-isis-out-of-america/.

9   Tim Gaynor, "Desert Hawks: Paramilitary Veterans Group
     Stakes Out US-Mexico Borderlands," *Al Jazeera America*,
     October 26, 2014, http://projects.aljazeera.com/2014/arizona-
     border-militia/.

10   John Lilyea, "Timothy Daniel Foley, 'Cartel Land' Star," *Valor
     Guardians* (blog), August 6, 2015, https://valorguardians.com/
     blog/?p=61221.

11   Movieclips Indie, "Cartel Land Official Trailer 1 (2015) - Drug
     Cartel Documentary HD," YouTube video, 2:30, June 3,
     2015, https://www.youtube.com/watch?v=xC5bpPfltOI&ab_
     channel=MovieclipsIndie.

12   Ryan Rifai, "Report: Islamophobia is a Multimillion-Dollar
     Industry," *Al Jazeera English*, June 24, 2016, https://www.
     aljazeera.com/features/2016/6/24/report-islamophobia-is-a-
     multimillion-dollar-industry.

13   Catherine Thompson, "Armed Anti-Muslim Activists Planned Protests in 20 Cities This Week," *Talking Points Memo*, October 8, 2015, https://talkingpointsmemo.com/muckraker/anti-muslim-global-rally-john-ritzheimer.

14   All quotes from Frazier and summary of his case are drawn from the criminal complaint: United States v. Parris Frazier, Robert Deatherage, Erik Foster, Case No. 15-7485MJ, US District Court for the State of Arizona, July 23, 2015, available at Outpost of Freedom (website), http://www.outpost-of-freedom.com/documents/Doc_01_Complaint.pdf.

15   United States v. Parris Frazier.

16   Rafael Carranza, "Border vigilantes, and the wall they might be watching." USA Today (AzCentral.com), https://www.usatoday.com/border-wall/story/vigilante-militia-patrol-us-mexico-border/559753001/.

17   U.S. District Court for the District of Arizona, United States of America v. Erik Stephen Foster, Case 2:15-cr-00924-GMS, PACER, 2019, page 1.

NOTES TO CHAPTER 5

1   Matt Shuham, "Border vigilante who slipped cops on the run found dead of apparent self-inflicted gunshot," Talking Points Memo, January 13, 2020, https://talkingpointsmemo.com/news/border-vigilante-who-slipped-cops-on-the-run-found-dead-of-apparent-self-inflicted-gun-shot.

2   Abby Mangel, "Brownsville: Texas border militants clash with the law (again)," *San Antonio Current*, November 3, 2014, https://www.sacurrent.com/the-daily/archives/2014/11/03/brownsville-texas-border-militants-clash-with-the-law-again.

3   KC Noneya, "Detaining Illegals," YouTube video, 0:29, October 13, 2014, https://www.youtube.com/watch?v=GoC5qlKL3hw&ab_channel=KcNoneya.

4   Intelligence Report, "Hate group expert Daniel Levitas discusses posse comitatus, Christian identity and more," Southern Poverty Law Center, June 15, 1998, https://www.splcenter.org/fighting-hate/intelligence-report/1998/hate-group-expert-daniel-levitas-discusses-posse-comitatus-christian-identity-movement-and.

5   Southern Poverty Law Center, "Sovereign Citizens Movement,"
     https://www.splcenter.org/fighting-hate/extremist-files/
     ideology/sovereign-citizens-movement.

6   J.J. MacNab, "'Sovereign' Citizen Kane," Southern Poverty Law
     Center, 2011, https://splcenter.org/sites/default/files/d6_legacy_
     files/ir_sov_special_report.pdf.

7   Bob Moser, "'Patriot' Shootout in Abbeville, S.C., Raises
     Questions about the Town's Extremist Past," Southern Poverty
     Law Center, April 20, 2004, https://www.splcenter.org/
     fighting-hate/intelligence-report/2004/%E2%80%98patriot
     %E2%80%99-shootout-abbeville-sc-raises-questions-about-
     town%E2%80%99s-extremist-past.

8   KC Noneya, "Border Patrol jamming up citizen patrol," YouTube
     video, 11:34, https://www.youtube.com/watch?v=fV3B0_
     WViT4&ab_channel=KcNoneya.

9   KC Noneya, "Busses," YouTube video, 6:36, October 10, 2014,
     https://www.youtube.com/watch?v=6-ah4nLyQ2M&ab_
     channel=KcNoneya.

10   KC Noneya, "BP Talking to Me," YouTube video, 29:03, May 15,
     2018, https://www.youtube.com/watch?v=zJXs-A6Z0Sc&ab_
     channel=KcNoneya.

11   Kevin Krause, "Feds Are Looking for Militia Man with 'Violent
     Tendencies' Who Mounted Armed Patrols on South Texas
     Border," *The Dallas Morning News*, August 9, 2019, https://www.
     dallasnews.com/news/crime/2019/08/09/feds-are-looking-for-
     militia-man-with-violent-tendencies-who-mounted-armed-
     patrols-on-south-texas-border/.

12   Krause, "Feds Are Looking for Militia Man."

13   David Neiwert, "'Camp Lonestar' Leader Arrested by ATF Agents
     for Firearms Violations," *Hatewatch* (blog), Southern Poverty
     Law Center, October 22, 2014, https://www.splcenter.org/hate
     watch/2014/10/22/%E2%80%98camp-lonestar%E2%80%99-
     leader-arrested-atf-agents-firearms-violations.

14   Thomas Korosec, "Cyberbunk," *Dallas Observer*, November
     21, 1996, https://www.dallasobserver.com/news/
     cyberbunk-6403188.

15   Aaron Nelsen, "Border Militia Members, Both Felons, Indicted
     on Gun Charges," *MySanAntonio*, November 4, 2014, https://
     www.mysanantonio.com/news/local/article/Border-militia-
     members-both-felons-indicted-on-5870390.php.

16   Joshua Fechter, "Militia Leader Posed with Greg Abbott Four
      Days Before Feds Found Ammonium Nitrate, Weapons at Hotel,"
      MySanAntonio, October 31, 2014, https://www.mysanantonio.
      com/news/local/politics/article/Photo-shows-Abbott-posing-
      with-militia-member-who-5860768.php.

17   Intelligence Report, "Border vigilante 'commander'
      charged after shooting incident," Southern Poverty
      Law Center, March 10, 2015, https://www.splcenter.org/
      fighting-hate/intelligence-report/2015/border-vigilante-
      %E2%80%98commander%E2%80%99-charged-after-
      shooting-incident.

18   Dane Schiller, "Borderland Militia Leader Heads to Federal
      Prison," *Houston Chronicle*, January 27, 2016, https://www.
      chron.com/news/houston-texas/article/Militia-member-heads-
      to-federal-prison-6788200.php.

19   Sarah Pruitt, "How Ruby Ridge and Waco Led to the Oklahoma
      City Bombing," History.com, May 22, 2018, updated April 2,
      2020, https://www.history.com/news/how-ruby-ridge-and-
      waco-led-to-the-oklahoma-city-bombing.

20   Bill Morlin, "FBI arrests blogger Gary Hunt for divulging
      informants' names," Southern Poverty Law Center
      (Hatewatch blog), April 12, 2017, https://www.splcenter.org/
      hatewatch/2017/04/12/fbi-arrests-blogger-gary-hunt-divulging-
      informants%E2%80%99-names.

21   Kevin Massey, "Massey – Letters from Jail #5," Outpost of
      Freedom, July 6, 2015, http://www.outpost-of-freedom.com/
      MasseyL05.htm.

22   Kevin Massey, "Massey – Letters from Jail #10," Outpost of
      Freedom, October 2, 2015, http://www.outpost-of-freedom.com/
      MasseyL10.htm.

23   Gary Hunt, "Camp Lone Star – Who is K. C. Massey?," *Outpost of
      Freedom* (blog), March 29, 2015, https://outpost-of-freedom.com/
      blog/?p=1087.

24   Kevin Massey, "Massey – Letters from Jail #1," Outpost of
      Freedom, June 27, 2015, http://www.outpost-of-freedom.com/
      MasseyL01.htm.

25   *United States of America v. James Russell Smith*, No. 3:19-CR-
      395-B, https://www.courtlistener.com/docket/16125332/united-
      states-v-smith/.

26   Bill Morlin, "Texas Border Militia Leader Sentenced to Prison," *Hatewatch* (blog), Southern Poverty Law Center, January 6, 2016, https://www.splcenter.org/hatewatch/2016/01/06/texas-border-militia-leader-sentenced-prison.

27   Kevin Krause, "Feds Are Looking for Militia Man."

28   Matt Shuham, "Wanted Border Vigilante Who Narrowly Escaped Capture Remains at Large," *Talking Points Memo*, August 9, 2019, https://talkingpointsmemo.com/news/border-vigilante-who-narrowly-escaped-capture-remains-at-large.

29   USA v. James Russell Smith.

30   Matt Shuham, "Wanted Border Vigilante."

31   Jack Herrera, "Armed Militias on the Border Have a Long—and Often Racist—History," *Pacific Standard*, April 22, 2019, https://psmag.com/news/armed-militias-on-the-border-have-a-long-and-often-racist-history.

32   Southern Poverty Law Center, "Knights of the Ku Klux Klan," https://www.splcenter.org/fighting-hate/extremist-files/group/knights-ku-klux-klan.

33   Brian MacQuarrie, "Militias' Era All But Over, Analysts Say," *The Boston Globe* (archive), April 19, 2005, http://archive.boston.com/news/nation/articles/2005/04/19/militias_era_all_but_over_analysts_say/.

34   Alyssa Newcomb, "Arizona Militia Leader and Candidate for Sheriff Killed Family During 911 Call," *ABC News*, May 3, 2012, https://abcnews.go.com/US/arizona-neo-nazi-sheriff-candidate-killed-family/story?id=16269803.

35   Curt Prendergast, "Prosecutors: Militia Member Had Gun-Making 'Factory' in His House," *Arizona Daily Star* (Tucson.com), August 28, 2019, updated August 29, 2019, https://tucson.com/news/local/prosecutors-militia-member-had-gun-making-factory-in-his-house/article_d8ef63ae-5512-547e-a293-88b9c44bdcf9.html.

36   Lindsey Bever, Kayla Epstein, and Eli Rosenberg, "Larry Hopkins Militia Group Planned to Kill Obama, Clinton and Soros, FBI Said," *The Washington Post*, April 23, 2019, https://www.washingtonpost.com/immigration/2019/04/23/militia-leader-border-said-members-were-training-kill-obama-clinton-soros-fbi-said/.

37   Mary Lee Grant and Nick Miroff, "U.S. Militia Groups Head to Border, Stirred By Trump's Call to Arms," *The Washington Post* (via *Texas Tribune*), November 4, 2018, https://www.texastribune.org/2018/11/04/us-militia-groups-head-border-stirred-trumps-call-arms/.

38   Southern Poverty Law Center, "SPLC Answers Questions About Antigovernment Extremists Who Detain Migrants Along the U.S.-Mexico Border," April 23, 2019, https://www.splcenter.org/news/2019/04/23/splc-answers-questions-about-antigovernment-extremists-who-detain-migrants-along-us-mexico.

39   "Reward Offered for 'Most Wanted' Fugitive Who May Be in Hunt County," *Herald-Banner*, July 25, 2019, updated July 26, 2019, https://www.heraldbanner.com/news/local_news/reward-offered-for-most-wanted-fugitive-who-may-be-in/article_6b84f136-af34-11e9-8f4c-53ae9bc5384d.html.

40   *Live PD* on A&E, "Help Us Find Kevin Massey!," Facebook post (video), October 17, 2019, https://www.facebook.com/watch/?v=772713693181653.

41   Bill Chappell, "Trump Pardons Ranchers Dwight And Steven Hammond Over 2012 Arson Conviction," *NPR*, July 10, 2018, https://www.npr.org/2018/07/10/627653866/president-trump-pardons-ranchers-dwight-and-steven-hammond-over-arson?t=1579973627878.

42   Kevin Krause, "North Texas Militia Vigilante Who Rounded Up Migrants at Border Found Dead After Months on the Run," *Dallas Morning News*, January 10, 2020, https://www.dallasnews.com/news/crime/2020/01/10/north-texas-militia-vigilante-who-rounded-up-migrants-at-border-found-dead-after-months-on-the-run/?fbclid=IwAR1ymUShPxWt25Fqrv1JYFX4SdqMQWAKbgjxRoQtxXxjAbmP2AaabENoaH8/.

43   Lynch Funeral Service, "Kevin 'KC' Massey, July 2, 1966 - December 23, 2019," January 3, 2020, https://www.lynchfuneralservice.com/obituary/kevin-massey.

44   Kevin Krause, "North Texas Militia Vigilante Who Rounded Up Migrants."

NOTES TO CHAPTER 6

1   Border Angels, "About Us," https://www.borderangels.org/about-us/.

2   Gabe Shivone, "Death as 'Deterrence': The Desert as a Weapon," Alliance for Global Justice, https://afgj.org/death-as-deterrence-the-desert-as-a-weapon.

3   "US-Mexico Border Migrant Deaths Rose in 2017 Even as Crossings Fell, UN Says," Agence France-Presse in Geneva (via The Guardian), February 6, 2018, https://www.theguardian.com/us-news/2018/feb/06/us-mexico-border-migrant-deaths-rose-2017.

4   All quotes from Trump's speech are drawn from the video recording on YouTube: James R. Daniels, "Donald Trump Full Speech In Phoenix, Arizona July 11, 2015 - 2016 Presidential Campaign Rally," YouTube video, 1:10:45, August 14, 2015, https://www.youtube.com/watch?v=HwRzPQAFNiM.

5   Jeremy Diamond, "David Duke on Trump: He's 'the Best of the Lot,'" CNN, August 25, 2015, https://www.cnn.com/2015/08/25/politics/david-duke-donald-trump-immigration/index.html.

6   Eugene Scott, "Trump Denounces David Duke, KKK," CNN, March 3, 2016, https://www.cnn.com/2016/03/03/politics/donald-trump-disavows-david-duke-kkk/index.html.

7   Yoni Appelbaum and Daniel Lombroso, "'Hail Trump!': White Nationalists Salute the President-elect," The Atlantic, November 21, 2016, https://www.theatlantic.com/politics/archive/2016/11/richard-spencer-speech-npi/508379/.

8   Sarah Bardon and Simon Carswell, "Trump hit by first diplomatic crisis over Mexico border wall," The Irish Times, January 26, 2017, https://www.irishtimes.com/news/world/us/trump-hit-by-first-diplomatic-crisis-over-mexico-border-wall-1.2952826.

9   Ben Zimmer, "Where Does Trump's 'Invasion' Rhetoric Come From?," The Atlantic, August 6, 2019, https://www.theatlantic.com/entertainment/archive/2019/08/trump-immigrant-invasion-language-origins/595579/.

10   Washington Office on Latin America (WOLA), "Fact Sheet: Why Central American Families are Fleeing their Homes," ReliefWeb, March 14, 2018, https://reliefweb.int/report/united-states-america/fact-sheet-why-central-american-families-are-fleeing-their-homes.

11   Cuffe, "'No Alternatives': Thousands Flee Honduras in US-Bound Caravan," *Al Jazeera English*, October 17, 2018, https://www.aljazeera.com/news/2018/10/17/no-alternatives-thousands-flee-honduras-in-us-bound-caravan.

12   Sandra Cuffe,"Honduran Survivor of Migrant Massacre Joins Caravan for Safety," *Al Jazeera English*, November 5, 2018, https://www.aljazeera.com/news/2018/11/5/honduran-survivor-of-migrant-massacre-joins-caravan-for-safety.

13   Patrick Strickland, "Guatemalans Sheltering in US Church Avoid Deportation," *Al Jazeera English*, October 28, 2016, https://www.aljazeera.com/features/2016/10/28/guatemalans-sheltering-in-us-church-avoid-deportation.

14   Strickland, "Guatemalans Sheltering in US Church."

15   Dara Lind, "The Migrant Caravan, Explained," *Vox*, October 25, 2018, https://www.vox.com/2018/10/24/18010340/caravan-trump-border-honduras-mexico.

16   Matthew Choi, "Trump: Military Will Defend Border from Caravan 'Invasion,'" *Politico*, October 29, 2018, https://www.politico.com/story/2018/10/29/trump-military-caravan-migrants-945683.

17   Sandra Cuffe, "After Resting in Mexico City, Caravan Ready to Continue North," *Al Jazeera English*, November 9, 2018, https://www.aljazeera.com/news/2018/11/9/after-resting-in-mexico-city-caravan-ready-to-continue-north.

18   Saeed Ahmed and Paul P. Murphy, "Here's What We Know So Far About Robert Bowers, the Pittsburgh Synagogue Shooting Suspect," *CNN*, October 28, 2018, https://www.cnn.com/2018/10/27/us/synagogue-attack-suspect-robert-bowers-profile/index.html.

19   Masha Gessen, "Why the Tree of Life Shooter Was Fixated on the Hebrew Immigrant Aid Society," *The New Yorker*, October 27, 2018, https://www.newyorker.com/news/our-columnists/why-the-tree-of-life-shooter-was-fixated-on-the-hebrew-immigrant-aid-society.

20   "Fox News Guest Claims Migrant Caravan Is Bringing 'Small Pox and Leprosy and TB That Is Going to Infect Our People,'" *Media Matters for America*, October 29, 2018, https://www.mediamatters.org/fox-news/fox-news-guest-claims-migrant-caravan-bringing-small-pox-and-leprosy-and-tb-going-infect.

21   Jessica Guynn, Brad Heath, and Matt Wynn, "How a Lie About George Soros and the Migrant Caravan Multiplied Online," *USA Today*, October 31, 2018, https://www.usatoday.com/in-depth/news/nation/2018/10/31/george-soros-and-migrant-caravan-how-lie-multiplied-online/1824633002/.

22   Ryan Devereaux, "Bodies in the Borderlands," *The Intercept*, May 4, 2019, https://theintercept.com/2019/05/04/no-more-deaths-scott-warren-migrants-border-arizona/.

23   Paul Ingram, "Feds Drop Case Against No More Deaths Volunteer Scott Warren," *Tuscon Sentinel*, February 27, 2020, https://www.tucsonsentinel.com/local/report/022620_warren_charge/feds-drop-case-against-no-more-deaths-volunteer-scott-warren/.

NOTES TO CHAPTER 7

1   KGUN9, "Underground Bunker Possibly Used for Human Trafficking of Children found in Tucson," YouTube video, 1:19, May 31, 2018, https://www.youtube.com/watch?v=IV_D1JJAhQM.

2   "Veterans on Patrol Discovers Disturbing Abandoned Camp in Tucson," *KOLD13*, June 1, 2018, updated June 4, 2018, https://www.kold.com/story/38322543/veterans-on-patrol-abandoned-camp-tucson/.

3   "Veterans on Patrol Discovers Disturbing Abandoned Camp in Tucson."

4   Child of God, "US Vets FIND Pedophile Child TRAFFICKING Camp in Arizona!," YouTube video, 4:57, https://www.youtube.com/watch?v=MSTp-36wPCQ.

5   Pima County Sheriff's Department's Facebook page. June 7, 2018, https://www.facebook.com/pimasheriff/posts/1969733403084277.

6   Ishmael N. Daro, "Claims of a 'Child Sex Camp' in Arizona Are Fueling the Latest Conspiracy Theory," *Buzzfeed News*, June 6, 2018, https://www.buzzfeednews.com/article/ishmaeldaro/how-a-homeless-camp-in-arizona-became-a-child-sex-camp.

7   Alicia Powe, "US Veterans Uncover Underground Bunker Possibly Used for Child Trafficking Camp in Arizona," *Gateway Pundit*, June 3, 2018, https://www.thegatewaypundit.com/2018/06/us-veterans-uncover-underground-bunker-possibly-used-for-child-trafficking-camp-in-arizona/.

8   Emma Parry, "'IT'S SICK' Sinister 'Child Sex Trafficking Camp' with 'Underground Jail for Kids', 'Rape Tree' and Name 'Maddie' Etched into Tree," *The Sun* (London), June 5, 2018, https://www.thesun.co.uk/news/6451966/sinister-child-sex-trafficking-camp-with-underground-jail-for-kids-rape-tree-and-name-maddie-etched-into-tree/.

9   Salvador Hernandez, "A Man Pushing A 'Child Sex Camp' Conspiracy Theory Has Been Arrested For Trespassing," *Buzzfeed News*, July 23, 2018, https://www.buzzfeednews.com/article/salvadorhernandez/a-man-pushing-a-child-sex-camp-conspiracy-theory-has-been.

10   Kelly House, "At Bundy Encampment, Outsider Says Militants 'Attacked' His Group," *Oregon Live*, January 7, 2016, https://www.oregonlive.com/pacific-northwest-news/2016/01/at_bundy_encampment_outsider_s.html.

11   Nick R. Martin, "Arizona Vigilante Michael Meyer of 'Veterans on Patrol' Arrested Amid Pizzagate-Style Conspiracy Theory," *Hatewatch* (blog), Southern Poverty Law Center, July 9, 2018, https://www.splcenter.org/hatewatch/2018/07/09/arizona-vigilante-michael-meyer-veterans-patrol-arrested-amid-pizzagate-style-conspiracy.

12   Curt Prendergast, "Armed Patrols Aim to Protect Homeless Vets, Women," *Arizona Daily Star* (Tucson.com), November 21, 2015, https://tucson.com/news/local/armed-patrols-aim-to-protect-homeless-vets-women/article_fbfe3644-f847-5218-803f-17869537bc97.html.

NOTES TO CHAPTER 8

1   Morgan Loew, "Border Town Takes Stand Against Militias," *AZFamily.com* (CBS 5), October 25, 2018, https://www.azfamily.com/news/investigations/cbs_5_investigates/border-town-takes-stand-against-militias/article_fb0eb244-d7ce-11e8-99fa-93e489605fd4.html.

2   Nick R. Martin, "Five Things You Should Know about the Upcoming 'Trump Unity Rally' in Arizona," Southern Poverty Law Center, March 9, 2018, https://www.splcenter.org/hatewatch/2018/03/09/5-things-you-should-know-about-upcoming-trump-unity-rally-arizona.

3   Megan Cassidy, "Trump rally in Phoenix Draws Arpaio,
     Ward – Plus Cheers and Jeers," The Republic (AZcentral.com),
     March 10, 2018, https://www.azcentral.com/story/news/local/
     phoenix/2018/03/10/trump-unity-rally-phoenix-draws-cheers-
     jeers-joe-arpaio/413682002/.

4   C-SPAN, "'Angel Families' on Illegal Immigration," September 7,
     2018, https://www.c-span.org/video/?451186-1/angel-families-
     illegal-immigration.

5   Jane Eppinga, "Murder at Ruby," *Arizona Capitol Times*, April 27,
     2012, https://azcapitoltimes.com/news/2012/04/27/murder-at-
     ruby/.

6   Scott Dyke, "Meandering the Mesquite: Bloody Ruby Storied
     Past at Western Ghost Town," *Green Valley News*, October 1,
     2016, https://www.gvnews.com/lifestyle/meandering-the-
     mesquite-bloody-ruby-storied-past-at-western-ghost-town/
     article_a49aad52-8738-11e6-a528-d788f9171637.html.

NOTES TO CHAPTER 9

1   Patrick Strickland, "Beyond Pizzagate: Anti-Immigrant
     Conspiracists Traffic Fear in Southern Arizona," *Political
     Research Associates,* October 13, 2020, https://www.
     politicalresearch.org/2020/10/13/beyond-pizzagate.

2   Jana Winter, "Exclusive: FBI Document Warns Conspiracy
     Theories Are a New Domestic Terrorism Threat," *Yahoo! News*,
     August 1, 2019, https://www.yahoo.com/now/fbi-documents-
     conspiracy-theories-terrorism-160000507.html.

3   Julia Carrie Wong, "Trump Referred to Immigrant 'Invasion' in
     2,000 Facebook Ads, Analysis Reveals," *The Guardian*, August
     5, 2019, https://www.theguardian.com/us-news/2019/aug/05/
     trump-internet-facebook-ads-racism-immigrant-invasion.

4   Tim Arango, Nicholas Bogel-Burroughs, and Katie Bennett,
     "Minutes Before El Paso Killing, Hate-Filled Manifesto Appears
     Online," *The New York Times*, August 3, 2019, https://www.
     nytimes.com/2019/08/03/us/patrick-crusius-el-paso-shooter-
     manifesto.html.

5   Eleanor Dearman, "Racism and the Aug. 3 Shooting: One
      Year Later, El Paso Reflects On the Hate Behind the Attack,"
      El Paso Times, July 29, 2020, updated August 1, 2020, https://
      www.elpasotimes.com/in-depth/news/2020/07/30/el-paso-
      walmart-shooting-community-reflect-racist-motive-behind-
      attack/5450331002/.

6   Norimitsu Onishi, "The Man Behind a Toxic Slogan Promoting
      White Supremacy," *The New York Times*, September 20, 2019,
      https://www.nytimes.com/2019/09/20/world/europe/renaud-
      camus-great-replacement.html.

7   Simon Romero, Manny Fernandez, and Mariel Padilla, "Massacre
      at a Crowded Walmart in Texas Leaves 20 Dead," *The New York
      Times*, August 3, 2019.

8   Michael Gold, "4 Arrested and 23 Guns Seized in Plot Against
      Muslim Enclave in Upstate N.Y.," *The New York Times*, January
      22, 2019, https://www.nytimes.com/2019/01/22/nyregion/
      islamberg-attack-muslim-community.html.

9   Amy Forliti, "2 Militia Members Admit Role in Attack on
      Minnesota Mosque," Associated Press, January 24, 2019, https://
      apnews.com/article/68c7fd8014424480932e663d73d46cc1.

NOTES TO CHAPTER 10

1   Antonia Noori Farzan, "He Was Kicked Out of a Border
      Militia. Then the FBI Found a Gun 'Factory' in His Home," *The
      Washington Post*, August 30, 2019, https://www.washingtonpost.
      com/nation/2019/08/30/border-militia-joshua-pratchard-gun-
      factory-fbi/.

2   Farzan, "He Was Kicked Out of a Border Militia."

3   Matt Shuham, "Failed Border Vigilante, Amateur Gunsmith
      Gets 75 Months in Federal Prison," *Talking Points Memo*, August
      28, 2019, https://talkingpointsmemo.com/news/failed-border-
      vigilante-amateur-gunsmith-gets-75-months-in-federal-prison.

4   Farzan, "He Was Kicked Out of a Border Militia."

5   Farzan, "He Was Kicked Out of a Border Militia."

6   Farzan, "He Was Kicked Out of a Border Militia."

7   Matt Shuham, "Failed Border Vigilante."

8   Matt Shuham, "Failed Border Vigilante."

9   Curt Prendergast, "Prosecutors: Militia Member Had Gun-Making 'Factory' in His House," *Arizona Daily Star* (Tucson. com), January 28, 2019, last modified February 3, 2021, https://tucson.com/news/local/prosecutors-militia-member-had-gun-making-factory-in-his-house/article_d8ef63ae-5512-547e-a293-88b9c44bdcf9.html.

10   Prendergast, "Prosecutors: Militia Member Had Gun-Making 'Factory.'"

NOTES TO CHAPTER 11

1   U.S. Customs and Border Protection, "BP Captures Convicted Sex Offender Near Arivaca," June 10, 2020, https://www.cbp.gov/newsroom/local-media-release/bp-captures-convicted-sex-offender-near-arivaca.

2   Adam Gabbatt, "Protests About Police Brutality Are Met with Wave of Police Brutality Across U.S.," *The Guardian*, June 6, 2020, https://www.theguardian.com/us-news/2020/jun/06/police-violence-protests-us-george-floyd.

3   WFTF Ministry #VOP, "Previously Deported Criminal in Route to Robles Elementary School Intercepted by VOP," YouTube video, 5:21, July 3, 2020, https://www.youtube.com/watch?v=LM56e4LkY-I&t=159s&ab_channel=WFTFMinistry%23VOP.

4   WFTF Ministry #VOP, "Screwy Louie & Hans Solo," YouTube video, 2:45, June 9, 2020, https://www.youtube.com/watch?v=3AdX6mNdQHM&ab_channel=WFTFMinistry%23VOP.

5   WFTF Ministry #VOP, "Cartel Dope Mine Shut Down," YouTube video, 3:57, April 22, 2020, https://www.youtube.com/watch?v=PzT9nyGCVkI&ab_channel=WFTFMinistry%23VOP.

6   Dan Patterson and Will Rahn, "What Is the QAnon Conspiracy Theory?," *CBS News*, March 29, 2021, https://www.cbsnews.com/news/what-is-the-qanon-conspiracy-theory/.

7   Bobby Allyn, "Twitter Removes Thousands of QAnon Accounts, Promises Sweeping Ban on the Conspiracy," *NPR*, July 21, 2020, https://www.npr.org/2020/07/21/894014810/twitter-removes-thousands-of-qanon-accounts-promises-sweeping-ban-on-the-conspir.

8   Alex Kaplan, "Here are the QAnon Supporters Running for Congress in 2020," *Media Matters for America*, January 7, 2020, https://www.mediamatters.org/qanon-conspiracy-theory/here-are-qanon-supporters-running-congress-2020.

9   Ben Collins and Brandy Zadrozny, "Facebook Bans QAnon Across its Platforms," *NBC News*, October 6, 2020, https://www.nbcnews.com/tech/tech-news/facebook-bans-qanon-across-its-platforms-n1242339.

10   Lois Beckett, "QAnon: A Timeline of Violence Linked to the Conspiracy Theory," *The Guardian*, October 16, 2020, https://www.theguardian.com/us-news/2020/oct/15/qanon-violence-crimes-timeline.

NOTES TO CHAPTER 12

1   Kahron Spearman, "Video Shows 4 Trump Supporters Assaulting Man Who Hit Their Truck with Flashlight," *Daily Dot*, November 3, 2020, https://www.dailydot.com/debug/trump-supporters-assaulting-man-tucson-video/.

2   Carol Ann Alaimo, "Tucson Police: Man Mistaken for Graffiti Vandal Dies in Election Day Clash," *Arizona Daily Star* (Tucson.com), November 6, 2020, updated December 30, 2020, https://tucson.com/news/local/crime-and-courts/tucson-police-man-mistaken-for-graffiti-vandal-dies-in-election-day-clash/article_ed92e2be-6203-52da-a42b-a9a9d4f60ccc.html.

3   "Crowd of Protesters in Phoenix Fired Up by Conspiracy Theorist Alex Jones," AZFamily.com (3TV, CBS 5), November 5, 2020, https://www.azfamily.com/news/politics/election_headquarters/crowd-of-protesters-in-phoenix-fired-up-by-conspiracy-theorist-alex-jones/article_dea394d0-1fe3-11eb-9a4b-93fa25a8ddc1.html.

4   Tim Nguyen and Mark Scott, "How 'SharpieGate' Went from Online Chatter to Trumpworld Strategy in Arizona," *Politico*, November 5, 2020, https://www.politico.com/news/2020/11/05/sharpie-ballots-trump-strategy-arizona-434372.

5   Christina Carrega, Veronica Stracqualursi, and Josh Campbell, "13 Charged in Plot to Kidnap Michigan Gov. Gretchen Whitmer," *CNN Politics*, October 8, 2020, https://www.cnn.com/2020/10/08/politics/fbi-plot-michigan-governor-gretchen-whitmer/index.html.

6   Lois Beckett, "Armed Protesters Demonstrate Against Covid-19 Lockdown at Michigan Capitol," *The Guardian*, April 30, 2020, https://www.theguardian.com/us-news/2020/apr/30/michigan-protests-coronavirus-lockdown-armed-capitol.

7   Chuck Goudie and Barb Markoff, "Disturbing New Details in Alleged Plot to Kidnap Michigan Governor Gretchen Whitmer," *ABC 7*, November 18, 2020, https://abc7chicago.com/michigan-governor-gretchen-whitmer-kidnapping-plot-militia/8079861/.

8   Staff and Agencies in Corinto, "Thousands of Migrants Cross into Guatemala with Slim Hopes of Reaching US," *The Guardian*, October 1, 2020, https://www.theguardian.com/world/2020/oct/01/honduran-migrant-caravan-cross-guatemala.

9   Julie Hirschfeld Davis and Michael D. Shear, "Shoot Migrants' Legs, Build Alligator Moat: Behind Trump's Ideas for Border," *The New York Times*, October 1, 2019, https://www.nytimes.com/2019/10/01/us/politics/trump-border-wars.html.

10   Michael Crowley, "Trump Denies Considering a Border Moat," *The New York Times*, October 2, 2019, https://www.nytimes.com/2019/10/02/us/politics/trump-alligator-snakes-moat.html.

11   Julián Aguilar, "Border Apprehensions Down Sharply in 2020 but Spiked in September," *The Texas Tribune*, October 14, 2020, https://www.texastribune.org/2020/10/14/texas-border-immigrants-apprehensions/.

12   Nick Miroff, "Immigration Arrests Along the Mexico Border Surged Again in October," *The Washington Post*, November 19, 2020, https://www.washingtonpost.com/immigration/border-arrests-surge-cctober-trump/2020/11/19/4155cf7a-2ab2-11eb-b847-66c66ace1afb_story.html.

NOTES TO THE CONCLUSION

1   Terry Sayles, Facebook, January 8, 2021, 10:33 a.m., https://www.facebook.com/photo?fbid=3493218657456299&set=g.375225756565077.

2   Charlie Savage, "Incitement to Riot? What Trump Told
    Supporters Before Mob Stormed Capitol," *The New York Times*,
    January 10, 2021, updated January 12, 2021, https://www.
    nytimes.com/2021/01/10/us/trump-speech-riot.html.

3   Jack Healy, "These Are the Five People Who Died in the Capitol
    Riot," *The New York Times*, January 11, 2021, updated February
    22, 2021, https://www.nytimes.com/2021/01/11/us/who-died-in-
    capitol-building-attack.html.

4   Peter Holley, "He Rioted at the Capitol. Then for Weeks He Lived
    in Luxury While Hiding From the FBI," *Texas Monthly*, February
    26, 2021, https://www.texasmonthly.com/news-politics/capitol-
    riots-luke-coffee/.

5   Simone Carter, "'Heil Hitler': Embattled Frisco Realtor Jenna
    Ryan Dropped from PayPal," *Dallas Observer*, January 26, 2021,
    https://www.dallasobserver.com/news/frisco-realtor-jenna-
    ryan-removed-from-paypal-other-fundraising-sites-11981736.

6   Todd C. Frankel, "A Majority of the People Arrested for Capitol
    Riot Had a History of Financial Trouble," *The Washington
    Post*, February 10, 2021, https://www.washingtonpost.com/
    business/2021/02/10/capitol-insurrectionists-jenna-ryan-
    financial-problems/.

7   CNN, "Trump Tells CPAC Crowd 'The Incredible Journey'
    Is 'Far From Being Over,'" *Channel3000*, February 28, 2021,
    https://www.channel3000.com/trump-tells-cpac-crowd-the-
    incredible-journey-is-far-from-being-over/.

8   Sky News, "IN FULL: Former US President Donald Trump
    Hints at 2024 Run," YouTube Video, 1:07:35, March 1, 2021,
    https://www.youtube.com/watch?v=KJTlo4bQL5c&ab_
    channel=SkyNews.

9   Sky News, "IN FULL: Former US President Donald Trump Hints
    at 2024 Run."

10 WFTF Ministry #VOP. "LEWIS ARTHUR ARRESTED!!!"
    YouTube video, 2:20, December 14, 2020, https://
    www.youtube.com/watch?v=Uiu3PtIjgvY&t=3s&ab_
    channel=WFTFMinistry%23VOP.

11 WFTF Ministry #VOP, "Children Crying in the Desert," YouTube
    video, 1:12:16, February 23, 2021, https://www.youtube.com/
    watch?v=avps_VCpLIs&ab_channel=WFTFMinistry%23VOP.

12   KTUL Staff, "Controversial Conference to End with Mask Burning Event in Broken Arrow," ABC-8 Tulsa, April 17, 2021, https://ktul.com/news/local/conservative-conference-to-end-with-mask-burning-event-in-broken-arrow.

13   Patriot News Network, "Health Freedom Conference," YouTube Video, 11:53:48, https://www.youtube.com/watch?v=QugG97XfXDc.

14   Ciara O'Rourke, "How Oath Keepers are Quietly Infiltrating Local Government," *Politico*, December 9, 2020, https://www.politico.com/news/magazine/2020/12/09/oath-keepers-far-right-group-infiltrate-local-government-texas-443773.

15   John Shirley, "Submission: Oath Keepers: An Insider's Perspective by John Shirley," *Hood County Today*, February 25, 2020, https://hoodcountytoday.com/oath-keepers-an-insiders-perspective/.

16   Curt Prendergast, "Busloads of Asylum Seekers Begin Arriving in Tucson as Biden Border Policies Take Effect," *Arizona Daily Star* (Tuscon.com), March 5, 2021, https://tucson.com/news/local/busloads-of-asylum-seekers-begin-arriving-in-tucson-as-biden-border-policies-take-effect/article_60b1bc4e-c26d-52ba-a8d2-5c4b13bfacee.html?fbclid=IwAR133ycf3AMbIOSSdxr9bo58oro8jtGpLwBQLJ8NOJmE__bOi2qfxX2rtxw.

17   Philip French, *Westerns* (New York: Viking Press, 1974), 12.

18   Simon Worrall, "Building Walls May Have Allowed Civilization to Flourish," *National Geographic*, October 5, 2018, https://www.nationalgeographic.com/science/article/wall-mexico-trump-book-talk-news.

INDEX

241

INDEX